ROMUALDO PACHECO'S CALIFORNIA!

THE MEXICAN~AMERICAN WHO WON

by LOREN NICHOLSON

CALIFORNIA HERITAGE PUBLISHING ASSOCIATES

CALIFORNIA HERITAGE SERIES

San Luis Obispo ~ 1990 ~ San Jose

Copyright 1990 by Loren Nicholson, San Luis Obispo, CA.

All rights reserved. No part of this book may be reproduced, in any form or by any means without permission from the author. However, book reviewers and researchers may use brief quotes as needed with appropriate reference to the book.

Printed in the United States.

ISBN 0-9623233-2-2
Library of Congress Catalog Card Number 90-083113

CALIFORNIA HERITAGE PUBLISHING ASSOCIATES, 156 Del Norte Way, San Luis Obispo, CA. 93405 and 1259 Camino Pablo, San Jose, CA 95125.

This book and those listed here may be ordered from the publisher at the address above.

RAILS ACROSS THE RANCHOS by Loren Nicholson. Hard Cover. $18.95 plus California sales tax in state.

OLD PICTURE POSTCARDS by Loren Nicholson. Soft Cover. $12.95 plus California sales tax in state.

ACKNOWLEDGMENTS

With deep appreciation, we offer thanks to California's librarians, museum directors, mission archival overseers and archival booksellers for allowing us to search through old documents and pour through nineteenth century books and periodicals looking for early prints produced from woodblocks and metal engravings.

We sought line prints depicting life and events occurring in California during Romualdo Pacheco's life. We found them and present what we believe to be a most fascinating collection. These illustrations also opened the way for us to tell the many "sidebar" stories about California during and after its transition from a territory of Mexico to an American state. Hopefully, these events also help explain the Americanization of an important person in western Ameican history.

```
          With special appreciation to Armand Zolezzi
          who commissioned this work.
```

✱

INTRODUCTION

Not all of the great pioneers of the west arrived in covered wagons or aboard ships. Some of them were born in the west and grew up in the presidios, mission settlements and pueblos of California and the Southwest.

The story of Romualdo Pacheco is the story of California during its nineteenth century move from a lonely, much neglected territory of Mexico to a raw, lawless state of the United States. An industrial revolution on the east coast was already underway when young Ramona Carrillo de Pacheco gave birth to her sons, Romualdo and Mariano, in the commandante's family quarters behind the deteriorating adobe and rock walls of the presidio at Santa Barbara.

By government decree, mission life was ending. Tough robust American, English and Scotch shipmasters roamed the California coast in sailing ships trading manufactured goods for hides and tallow from the ranchos. Some of these men took Mexican citizenship, accepted the catholic faith, married California women and sought land grants from the Mexican territorial government. They helped pave the way for later American military occupation. Some of them, like Shipmaster John Wilson, served as stepfathers to half-orphaned Mexican children like Romualdo and Mariano.

In this book, we proudly introduce Romualdo Pacheco to Americans of the twentieth and the coming twenty-first century. He grew up quietly to take a significant place in California statesmanship during a time of epidemic racial intolerance, surpassing most of California's new anglo population in the race for recognition. Through astute political action, he gradually positioned himself so that he came to serve as the 12th governor of California in the American period. Without bravado or boosting, Pacheco lived and died a hero of his people.

*

THE MEXICAN-AMERICAN WHO WON

CONTENTS

Page

Acknowledgments...................................3

Introduction......................................4

Illustrations.....................................6

The Joaquin Carrillo Family of San Diego...........8

Romualdo Pacheco's California!....................9

Ramona Carrillo Pacheco- Sidebar 1................13

War With Mexico in California- Sidebar 2..........22

California's Vigilance Committees- Sidebar 3......31

The Donner Party- Sidebar 4.......................35

The 1849 Gold Rush- Sidebar 5.....................37

California's Indians- Sidebar 6...................44

Pueblo de Los Angeles- Sidebar 7..................66

Building the Central Pacific Railroad- Sidebar 8..75

The Chinese in California- Sidebar 9..............84

Choosing California's Capital City- Sidebar 10...106

ROMUALDO PACHECO'S CALIFORNIA

ILLUSTRATIONS

COVER-Raising the American Flag at the Custom House in Monterey in 1846. Drawing by Jo Mora. Taken from an original plate owned by the author.

BACK COVER-Montgomerey Street looking north from California Street, San Francisco, 1854. (Annals of San Francisco)
THE JOAQUIN CARRILLO FAMILY OF SAN DIEGO.................8
SAN DIEGO HARBOR, 1830.................10
PUEBLO AND PRESIDIO OF SANTA BARBARA.................11
POPULATION OF CALIFORNIA WHEN ROMUALDO PACHECO WAS BORN.12
RAMONA CARRILLO DE PACHECO DE WILSON.................13
MISSION SANTA BARBARA.................14
A FULL-SAIL TRADING SHIP OF THE 1830'S.................15
A FULL-SAIL BRIG FLYING AMERICAN COLORS.................16
THE DE LA GUERRA CASA IN SANTA BARBARA.................17
A TRADING SHIP OFF THE ISLAND OF OAHU IN THE SANDWICH ISLANDS WHERE ROMUALDO PACHECO ATTENDED SCHOOL.........18
TROPICAL FOLIAGE OF EARLY OAHU ISLAND.................19
SPELLING AND READING BOOK ISSUED BY THE OAHU MISSION IN 1845.................20

OAHU CHARITY SCHOOL ATTENDED BY ROMUALDO PACHECO, HIS BROTHER AND OTHER CALIFORNIA BOYS.................20
ENGLISH ALPHABET CHART WITH HAWAIIAN SOUND TRANSLATIONS.21
SEAMAN'S CHAPEL AT OAHU.................22
JOHN FREMONT IN CALIFORNIA.................23
COMMODORE ROBERT STOCKTON.................25
CAPTAIN JOHN SUTTER.................26
SUTTERS FORT.................26
PORTRAITS-MARIANO VALLEJO AND THOMAS LARKIN.................27
PORTRAIT-JACOB LEESE.................28
FIRST BUILDING AT YERBA BUENA (SAN FRANCISCO).................28
PORTRAIT-SAM BRANNON AND HIS HOUSE AT YERBA BUENA (SAN FRANCISCO.................29
OLIVE GROVES AT MISSION SAN LUIS OBISPO.................30
VIGILANTE HANGING AT SAN FRANCISCO.................31
VIGILANTE HANGING AT SAN FRANCISCO.................32
NEWS OF CALIFORNIA PONY EXPRESS-California Star, 1847...33
THE DONNER PARTY.................34
DISSOLUTION OF JOHN WILSON-JAMES SCOTT PARTNERSHIP......36
1849 GOLD RUSH-.................37

CRADLE ROCKING FOR GOLD.................38
JOHN WILSON SERVED AS TREASURER IN SAN LUIS OBISPO......39
ROMUALDO PACHECO LEADS POSSE TO CAPTURE BANDITS.........40
SAN LUIS OBISPO MISSION SETTLEMENT-October, 1871........41
ADOBE CASA, PECHO Y ISLAY GRANT, SAN LUIS OBISPO........42
ADOBE CASA, CANADA DE LOS OSOS GRANT, SAN LUIS OBISPO...43
CALIFORNIA INDIANS-GATHERING ACORNS, SPEARING FISH......44
CALIFORNIA INDIANS AS DEPICTED BY 19TH CENTURY ARTISTS..46
CALIFORNIA INDIANS AS HUNTERS AND HOMEMAKERS...........47
A VAQUERO WITH WHIP-.................48
PUEBLO MONTEREY AND SAN CARLOS DE CARMELO MISSION.......49
MAP OF SAN FRANCISCO, 1854-51.................51
GOLDEN GATE AND FORT POINT, 1854.................52

THE MEXICAN-AMERICAN WHO WON

MISSION SAN FRANCISCO DE ASIS AND EARLY PRIEST, 1854....53
YERBA BUENA COVE IN 1849 AS GOLD RUSH BEGAN AND A SAN FRANCISCO SCENE, 1854..........................54
SAN FRANCISCO'S CITY HALL, 1851, AND BIG FIRE OF 1851...55
PORTSMOUTH SQUARE, CUSTOM HOUSE, AND POSTOFFICE, SAN FRANCISCO, 1854..........................56
MID-19TH CENTURY STREET SCENES IN SAN FRANCISCO, 1854...57
FANCY BALL AND WOMEN OF SAN FRANCISCO, 1854............58
WINN'S BRANCH RESTAURANT AND THE EL DORADO SALOON, 1854.59
ST. MARY'S CHURCH-Romualdo Pacheco and Mary McIntire were married here............................60
19TH CENTURY BRIDE......................61
CALIFORNIA STEAM NAVIGATION COMPANY POSTER..............62
PADDLEWHEELER LEAVES SAN FRANCISCO FOR SACRAMENTO.......63
CALIFORNIA-OREGON STAGE COACH BROADSIDE.................64
EL PUEBLO DE LA REINA DE LOS ANGELES, 1781..............65
MID-19TH CENTURY PORT OF STOCKTON......................68
VIEW OF SACRAMENTO CITY LANDING IN 1851.................69
FRONT STREET, SACRAMENTO................................70

PONY EXPRESS MAIL LEAVING SACRAMENTO FOR MISSOURI.......71
1850'S STREET SCENE IN SACRAMENTO.......................72
STRAIT OF MAGELLAN NEAR PUNTA ARENAS, 1872.............73
MAY 8, 1869- POSTER CELEBRATING COMPLETION OF TRANSCONTINENTAL RAILROAD, 1872.........................74
CENTRAL PACIFIC TRAIN IN SIERRA-NEVADA SNOWSHED, 1872...75
1872 EXTERIOR SCENES OF SIERRA-NEVADA SNOWSHEDS AND SNOW PLOW ENGINE, 1872.......................77
GEORGE PULLMAN, DEVELOPER AND PRINCIPAL EXECUTIVE OF LUXURIOUS RAILROAD PASSENGER CARS, 1872.................79
PULLMAN'S ELEGANT DINING CARS SERVED 40 PASSENGERS,1872-80
SLEEPING BERTHS ABOARD PULLMAN CARS, 1872...............81
VICTORIAN DECORATED PULLMAN PALACE CAR, 1872............82
KITCHEN AND DINING CAR OF UNION PACIFIC RAILROAD, 1872..83
A CHINESE MINER, MERCHANT AND COOLIE, AND GAMBLING DEN, 1854..................................84
CHINESE PEOPLE ON THE STREETS OF SAN FRANCISCO, 1854....85
POLITICAL CARTOON IN SAN FRANCISCO CHRONICLE,1871.......86
AUGUST 13, 1871- POLITICAL CARTOON......................87

POLITICAL CARTOON IN SAN FRANCISCO CHRONICLE............88
AUGUST 20, 1871-POLITICAL CARTOON......................89
JULY 23, 1871-POLITICAL CARTOON........................90
AUGUST 27, 1871-POLITICAL CARTOON......................91
EDITH STANTON AND SUSAN ANTHONY, JULY, 1871.............92
CALIFORNIA REPUBLICAN STATE TICKET, 1871................93
SAN FRANCISCO CATHOLICS CELEBRATED ANNIVERSARY OF POPE..94
INAUGURUAL BALL HELD IN NEW CAPITOL BUILDING............95
LIEUTENANT GOVERNOR ROMUALDO PACHECO AT SENATE MEET.....96
GOVERNOR NEWTON BOOTH ELECTED U.S. SENATOR.............97
1875-ROMUALDO PACHECO SWORN IN AS GOVERNOR.............98
RECALLING GOVERNOR ROMUALDO PACHECO'S BEGINNINGS.......102
RECALLING ROMUALDO PACHECO WORKING WITH VAQUEROS.......103
RECALLING THE DAYS OF WOODEN-WHEELED CARRETAS..........104
RECALLING CALIFORNIA'S TRADITIONAL RODEOS.............105
SAN JOSE-CALIFORNIA'S FIRST CAPITOL, 1849-51...........106
VALLEJO-CALIFORNIA'S SECOND CAPITOL, 1852-53...........107
BENICIA-CALIFORNIA'S THIRD CAPITOL, 1853-54. 108
SACRAMENTO-CALIFORNIA'S PRESENT CAPITOL, 1869-PRESENT..109

ROMUALDO PACHECO'S CALIFORNIA

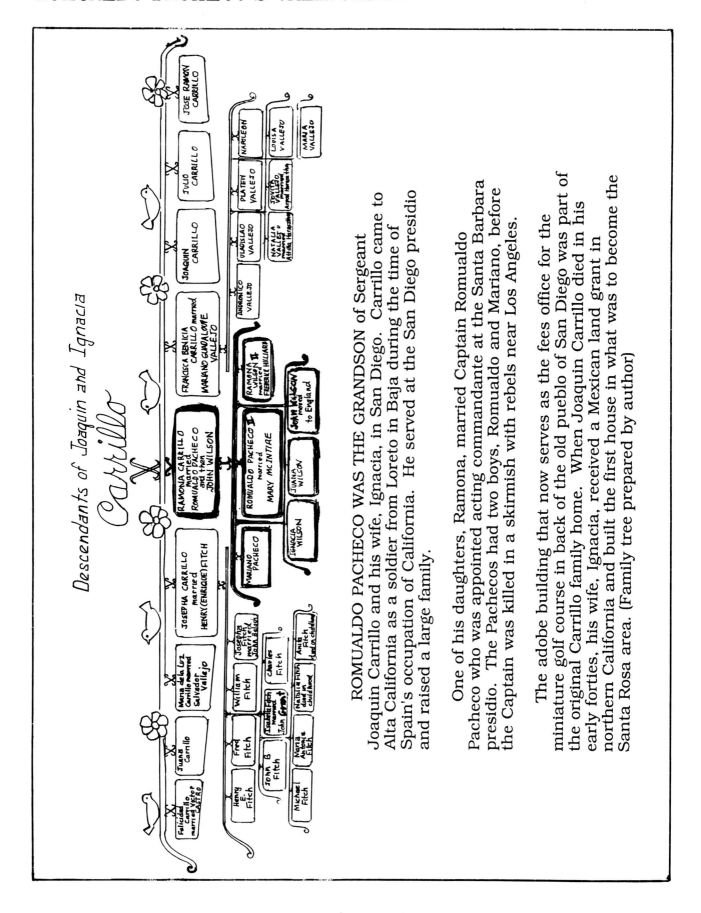

ROMUALDO PACHECO WAS THE GRANDSON of Sergeant Joaquin Carrillo and his wife, Ignacia, in San Diego. Carrillo came to Alta California as a soldier from Loreto in Baja during the time of Spain's occupation of California. He served at the San Diego presidio and raised a large family.

One of his daughters, Ramona, married Captain Romualdo Pacheco who was appointed acting commandante at the Santa Barbara presidio. The Pachecos had two boys, Romualdo and Mariano, before the Captain was killed in a skirmish with rebels near Los Angeles.

The adobe building that now serves as the fees office for the miniature golf course in back of the old pueblo of San Diego was part of the original Carrillo family home. When Joaquin Carrillo died in his early forties, his wife, Ignacia, received a Mexican land grant in northern California and built the first house in what was to become the Santa Rosa area. (Family tree prepared by author)

THE MEXICAN-AMERICAN WHO WON

ROMUALDO PACHECO'S CALIFORNIA!

Death in Cahuenga Canyon

When the governor's small military escort saw the rebel band from the South appear on a rise in Cahuenga Canyon that December day in 1831, they drew their mounts to an abrupt halt and waited. At least one hundred dust-covered men on horseback rode toward them.

Some of the governor's guard wanted to turn back. They knew they were no match for the revolutionaries. But Lt. Col. Manuel Victoria, the new governor of Alta California, was too filled with his mission of peace to make a judgment.

Among all of those revolutionaries, he did not see Jose Maria Avila leave the trail and take a flank position in the brush. He did not want to take these men seriously. He certainly did not suspect anyone of wanting to kill him. He only wanted to arrange a peaceful settlement.

The governor's musket still hung from his saddle when Avila rushed from the brush with lance at-the-ready. The governor may have caught the hatred in the rebel's eyes. He certainly heard the shouts of alarm from his men. But everything came too late, too unexpectedly. He suddenly felt the excruciating pain; the digging twisting iron lance in his side.

Captain Romualdo Pacheco, leader of the governor's military escort, crowded between Avila and Victoria. He fired his single-shot musket, then struck the rebel in the

ROMUALDO PACHECO'S CALIFORNIA

groin with the butt of his weapon. Avila was hit, but an intense fierceness kept him alive and strong for a few more minutes.

The force of Avila's heavy iron lance ripped Captain Pacheco's leather jacket. It plunged through his rib cage and tore at his lungs. Blood soaked the young captain's breast as he fell under frenzied hooves of a dozen soldier's horses crowding the trail.

As quickly as the skirmish started, it ended. The rebels, afraid now, backed away, turned, and rode hard for Pueblo de Los Angeles.

Captain Pacheco, acting commandante at the Santa Barbara Presidio, was dead. So was the rebel, Avila.

Victoria's men reassembled and carried the governor to Mission San Gabriel. Months followed while the women of the compound nursed him back to health. Then, in early 1832, former Governor Jose Echeandia's men put Victoria aboard the Mexican barque Pocahontas anchored in the bay at San Diego, and the ship carried him back to San Blas.(1)

In that brief skirmish along the trail, the new government of Manuel Victoria ended. It had started in March, 1830, when the Congress in Mexico City appointed him. Now, with Victoria gone from California, a bloodless power struggle took place between Pio Pico and Jose Echeandia, but Pico quickly succumbed, and Jose Echeandia regained the governorship.

Within a year, the law of the land changed. In 1833, the

SAN DIEGO HARBOR, 1830- In 1832, Governor Manuel Victoria sailed from San Diego aboard the Mexican barque Pocohontos, and Jose Echeandia regained the governorship of California. (Alfred Robinson, Life in California, 1846)

THE MEXICAN-AMERICAN WHO WON

PUEBLO AND PRESIDIO SANTA BARBARA from the harbor. Romualdo Pacheco's father was acting commandante of the presidio here. (Alfred Robinson, Life in California, 1846)

government decreed that the vast land holdings of the Catholic Church in Alta California must be granted to individuals, both Californios and Indians. The missions would be secularized and the duties of the padres limited to that of parish priests.(1)(2)

But what of Captain Romualdo Pacheco's family? His wife and sons? Their lives were forever changed too.

****

A Time of Grief and Healing

The women of Pueblo de Santa Barbara gathered in the commandante's apartment next to the presidio chapel. They surrounded 19-year-old Ramona Carrillo de Pacheco and her sons with their tears and compassion. They held and coddled little Mariano, just learning to walk, and, as was the custom when a mother was dry, one of the other mothers opened the front of her dress and breast-fed newborn Romualdo.

What was to happen to Ramona and her children? She could not remain in this presidio apartment. A new acting commandante and his family would soon occupy it. Besides, this military compound was no place for a young and beautiful woman alone.

That brief battle in Cahuenga Canyon had violated the destiny of a most promising family.

Day after day, Ramona could walk the winding path through the pueblo past orchards and small

Page 14 please

ROMUALDO PACHECO'S CALIFORNIA

POPULATION OF THE COUNTRY.

NAMES OF THE JURISDICTIONS, MISSIONS AND TOWNS.	PEOPLE OF ALL CLASSES AND AGES.				
	Men.	Women.	Boys.	Girls.	Total.
Jurisdiction of San Francisco.					
PRESIDIO OF SAN FRANCISCO	124	85	89	73	371
Town of San José de Guadalupe	166	145	103	110	524
Mission of San Francisco Solano	285	242	88	90	705
" of San Rafael	406	410	105	106	1027
" of San Francisco	146	65	13	13	237
" of Santa Clara	752	491	68	60	1371
" of San José	823	659	100	145	1727
" of Santa Cruz	222	94	80	20	366
Jurisdiction of Monterey.					
PRESIDIO OF MONTEREY	311	190	110	97	708
Village of Branciforte	52	34	27	17	130
Mission of San Juan Bautista	480	351	85	71	987
" of San Carlos	102	79	34	21	236
" of Na. Sa. de la Soledad	210	81	23	20	334
" of San Antonio	394	209	51	17	671
" of San Miguel	349	292	46	61	748
" of San Luis Obispo	211	103	8	7	329
Jurisdiction of Santa Barbara.					
PRESIDIO OF SANTA BARBARA	167	120	162	164	613
Mission of La Purissima	151	218	47	34	450
" of Santa Ines	142	136	82	96	456
" of Santa Barbara	374	267	51	70	762
" of Buenaventura	383	283	66	59	791
" of San Fernando	249	226	177	181	833
Town of La Reyna de los Angeles	552	421	213	202	1388
Jurisdiction of San Diego.					
PRESIDIO OF SAN DIEGO	295	1911	683	621	*5686
Mission of San Gabriel	574				
" of San Juan Capistrano	464				
" of San Luis Rey	1138				
" of San Diego	750	520	162	143	1575
Totals	10272	7632	2623	2498	23025

IN 1831, the year Romualdo Pacheco was born, Alexander Forbes, author of "History of Upper and Lower California", estimated the population of Alta California to be 23,025. According to his calculations, Indians made up 18,683 of the total; presidio soldiers, mission priests, craftsmen and free Spanish people living in mission settlements and pueblos made up another 4,342 people. (Annals of San Francisco, 1854)

THE MEXICAN-AMERICAN WHO WON

SIDEBAR STORY 1

RAMONA CARRILLO PACHECO

BEAUTIFUL AND NOBLE in bearing as a young woman, Ramona Carrillo was born in San Diego as the second child of Mexican military Sergeant Joaquin Carrillo and Ignacia Lugo Carrillo. Ramona married Romualdo Pacheco, a young engineering officer who had arrived in California in 1826 from Guanajuato, Mexico. He started as an aide to Governor Jose Echeandia.

When her husband was suddenly killed in the rebel uprising that culminated in Cahuenga Canyon, she was still a teenager, now with two children. Mariano was one-year old. Romualdo was one-month old.

In 1837, she received a 48,000-acre land grant on the Santa Maria River, the future border between Santa Barbara and San Luis Obispo Counties.

There is a legend about her courageous stand before Col. John Fremont at Mission San Luis Obispo to save the life of her cousin, Jose Jesus Pico, the local justice of the peace. Her effort succeeded, and Pico served beside Fremont until General Kearney had Fremont arrested and taken to Washington D.C. to stand military trial.

Ramona's second marriage to Shipmaster John Wilson from Dundee, Scotland assured her and her boys wealth and the good life that accompanied it. She had four more children with Wilson.

ROMUALDO PACHECO'S CALIFORNIA

EARLY MISSION SANTA BARBARA- Chumash Indians lived in one-room adobe casas to the left of the mission. The lavendaria in front of the mission where the Indian women washed their clothes was fed by tiled irrigation ditches from springs in the mountains.

from page 11
herds of cattle, up the hill to Mission Santa Barbara. She could see the smoke of fires from the adobe beehive-shaped ovens in the Chumash Indian village to the west of the church building, and she could watch the Indian women washing clothes in the mission lavadero, a place into which water flowed from the red tile viaduct constructed in Mission Canyon.

Some of the women hung their heads, not knowing how to greet the commandante's widow. Others nodded with understanding. There was nothing that anyone could do to bring the young Mexican woman's husband back to this earthly existence.

Because Captain Pacheco had been buried along the trail near Los Angeles, there was no kissing his handsome, dark-bearded face, no closing of Ramona's life with him except in lonely ceremony: lighting candles in the cold semi-darkness of the church sanctuary, bending in kneed prayer before the altar.

Perhaps Maria Antonia Carrillo de la Guerra y Noriega spoke to her husband on behalf of Ramona and her sons. In any case, Don Jose, the unquestioned patron of the pueblo, invited Ramona to come live with his large family in their spacious and well-kept adobe casa on the plaza. Ramona surely knew there could be no better place in all California for her boys to live and grow.(3)

So, the earliest memories of both Mariano and Romualdo included fiestas and social events at La Casa de la Guerra and the nearby casa of Ramona's cousin, Carlos Antonio de Jesus Carrillo. Guerra was Spanish. This fact prevented him from holding high political

THE MEXICAN-AMERICAN WHO WON

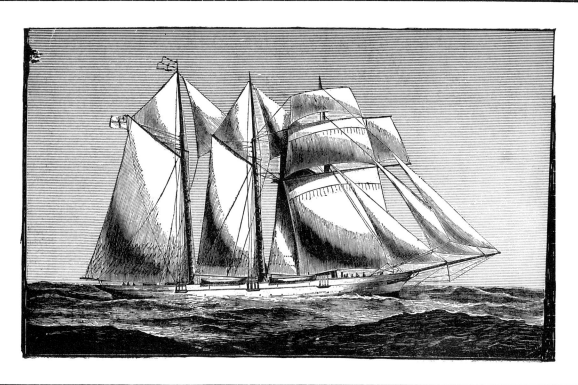

WHEN JOHN WILSON married Ramona Carrillo de Pacheco in 1835, he and his partner, James Scott, owned the Ayacucho, the fastest trading vessel along the California coast. (Richard Dana, "Two Years Before the Mast," 1836)

positions in Mexican California. However, it didn't stop him from using his substantial power and influence in helping his brother-in-law, Don Carlos.

Don Carlos became a prominent politician and leader in the territory. He not only served as Alta California's representative to the Congress in Mexico City during 1831-32, but in 1837 received a short-lived appointment as California's governor.(4)

Perhaps without knowing it, young Romualdo Pacheco saw the successes of his many cousins and was filled with their aspirations. That may have been the beginning of the fire in his heart; the beginning of the dreams and hopes that guided him. The Guerra home must have also provided a unique atmosphere for his young widowed mother. She could not help but be aware of the impressive status and affluence enjoyed by the women of these families most of whom married Americans and other anglo men, nearly all of them arriving in Mexican-California by way of trading ships.

She could watch and consider. Her own eldest sister, Josepha, in San Diego, had married Henry Fitch, a trader and shipper from Massachusetts (5). And clearly, Don Carlos Carrillo welcomed the foreigners who sought marriage with his daughters.

Encarnacion married Thomas Robbins of Massachusetts; Josepha married William Goodwin Dana, a cousin of Richard Henry Dana, also from Massachusetts; Francisca

ROMUALDO PACHECO'S CALIFORNIA

FULL-SAIL TRADING vessels operated by Europeans and Americans sailed the Pacific from Callao and Valparaiso to the Sandwich Islands and back along the California coast in a great triangle.

married A. B. Thompson from Maine; Manuela married John C. Jones from Boston; and Antonia married Lewis Burton from Tennessee.(6)

In the Guerra home, Ramona attended the wedding of Teresa de Jesus when she married W.E.P. Hartnell from Lancashire, England; and Maria de las Augustias, who first married Manuel Jimeno Casarin, a Mexican, and then Dr. J. D. Ord, a native of Maryland; and Ana Maria's marriage to Alfred Robinson from Massachusetts.

Their husbands became members of the Catholic Church and enjoyed the influence of their fathers-in-law who helped them obtain large land grants in the territory.

This extraordinary mix of marriages created a virtual melting pot of hispanic-anglo children, and the quiet influence of these women in their time and place cannot be underestimated. Such a cross-cultural relationship of cousins, aunts and uncles foretold the future for Ramona's sons, and made what happened next a natural occurrence.

Ramona, now 22 years old, met Shipmaster John Wilson, a Scotsman from Dundee.

A New Love For Ramona

Don Jose de la Guerra welcomed traders in his home. He not only bought and sold large amounts of goods on his own behalf, but often represented the mission priests in trade and financial matters.

Perhaps it was during one of these visits that Captain Wilson met Ramona and was immediately

THE MEXICAN-AMERICAN WHO WON

smitten by her. He spoke to her protector about courting her, getting permission to walk with her on the plaza and along the beach. He brought her gifts from the wealth of manufactured goods aboard his barque. Four years had passed since the death of her husband. Ramona may have been cautious, or even afraid, but her eyes sparkled again. She gave even more care to the sweep of her long dark hair drawn tightly across her ears, making a silken roll at the back of her head. New color came to her cheeks, contrasting brightly with her earrings, her necklace and her jangling bright bracelets on both arms.

In the interval before the marriage, Mariano and Romualdo became acquainted with the man who proposed marriage to their mother, and became enthralled with the stories about his adventures as a shipmaster.

Both Wilson and his partner, James Scott, were tough, strong men. They had reached the Pacific as young sailors out of Scotland, sailing the Atlantic Ocean and then making the treacherous trip through the Strait of Magellan and up the coast to Valparaiso. Several traders from Boston and European ports used this port to trade manufactured goods for hides and tallow from California, as well as goods that found their way from Canton and Manila via the Sandwich Islands.

CASA DE LA GUERRA, Santa Barbara- After her first husband's death, Ramona Pacheco was invited to bring her boys to live in the household of Jose de la Guerra y Noriega, the unquestioned patron of the pueblo. (Sketch by Bernice Loughran-Nicholson)

ROMUALDO PACHECO'S CALIFORNIA

Wilson first arrived on the California coast in 1826, serving as master of the Brig Thomas Nowlan. A few years later, he and his partner began their own trading business with the purchase of the Brig Ayacucho. Traders in California considered their vessel the fastest on the coast.

Through the years, the partners purchased other vessels and operated a small fleet in the Pacific. They sailed into ports, large and small, and when necessary, rented horses and rode into the interior, buying hides and tallow in California, taking consignments and trading their wares. The deck of their ship often served as a general store where people purchased cloth, shoes, spices, handplows and dozens of other manufactured items.(7)

Through Richard Henry Dana's book, Two Years Before the Mast, we learn a great deal about Wilson. He was "..a short, active well-built man," Dana said.

Once, when the Pilgrim, the ship Dana sailed aboard, drifted out of control in the wind at San Diego, Wilson came to the rescue. After seeing Wilson in action during that experience, Dana painted him as a somewhat heroic man, and gave

OAHU, SANDWICH ISLANDS- When Romualdo Pacheco was five years old, he and his brother were sent to the Missionary Charity School in the Sandwich Islands to begin their education.
(Robert Dampier, To the Sandwich Islands on HMS Blonde, 1825)

THE MEXICAN-AMERICAN WHO WON

THE SANDWICH ISLANDS were part of a great Pacific trading triangle where importers-exporters set up near the beaches to meet incoming ships carrying goods.
(Robert Dampier, "To the Sandwich Islands on HMS Blonde", 1825)

reports of his activities in other California ports.(8) Through letters sent by traders stationed at various locations in the great Pacific triangle including South America, Mexico, California and the Sandwich Islands, there is additional valuable literature describing the man who became husband to Ramona and stepfather to Mariano and Romualdo.(9)

To make his request for Ramona's hand legal, Wilson took Mexican citizenship and joined the Catholic Church. In Dana's sequel to his book, he recalls the wedding at Santa Barbara. The sounds of guitars and violins and the dancing and the fiesta on the plaza in front of Guerra's casa all became part of the memories of Dana in California.

Wilson's love for Ramona and the boys showed itself in many ways. Soon after their marriage, he bought the large adobe casa of Daniel Hill on present-day Carrillo Street in Santa Barbara. Hill was a Massachusett's man with a wide reputation as a builder.(10)

The Wilson family casa social environment soon matched that of the Guerra residence. There are many references to Ramona as a strikingly attractive woman hosting California governors, well-known American and European travelers and many of Wilson's trader friends. This special place in the community helped teach Ramona's boys how to move with ease among men of all walks of life. Their mother must

ROMUALDO PACHECO'S CALIFORNIA

have known she was preparing them for important places in life. Young Romualdo could feel assured about his dreams.(11)(12)

A School Far From Home

Soon after their marriage, the Wilson's became concerned about the education of the boys. Since there was so little opportunity for a dependable and continuing education for children in Mexican California, Wilson sought a most unorthodox solution.

In 1838, he put Romualdo and Mariano aboard a sailing vessel bound for the Sandwich Islands, over 3,000 miles from home. From Wilson's trading activities on the island of Oahu, he already knew Andrew and Rebecca Worth Johnstone. Johnstone, like Wilson, was born in Dundee, Scotland, and

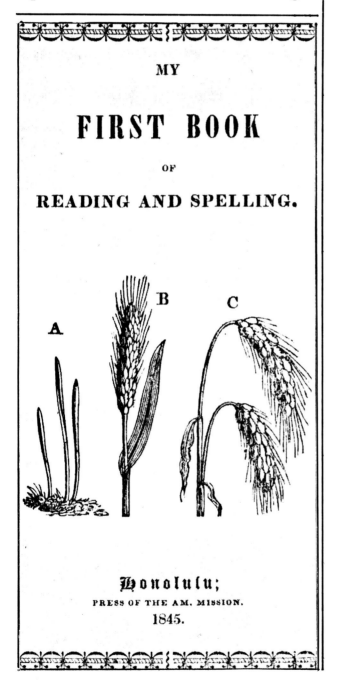

LEFT: The American missionaries produced some of their own books such as this one for reading and spelling.

BELOW: The Oahu Charity School which Romualdo and a group of other California boys attended. It was supported largely by seamen who visited the port and often left prodigy whose mothers were natives. (Missionary Album, Sesquicentennial Edition, 1820-1970)

THE MEXICAN-AMERICAN WHO WON

THE ALPHABET.

VOWELS.		SOUND.	
Names.		Ex. in Eng.	Ex. in Hawaii.
A a	â	as in *father*,	la—sun.
E e	a	— *tete*,	hemo—cast off.
I i	e	— *marine*,	marie—quiet.
O o	o	— *over*,	ono—sweet.
U u	oo	—*rule*,	nui—large.

CONSONANTS.	Names.	CONSONANTS.	Names.
B b	be	N n	nu
D d	de	P p	pi
H h	he	R r	ro
K k	ke	T t	ti
L l	la	V v	vi
M m	mu	W w	we

The following are used in spelling foreign words:

| F f | fe | S s | se |
| G g | ge | Y y | yi |

Rebecca came from Massachusetts. They originally arrived at Oahu under sponsorship of the American Board of Commissioners for Foreign Missions, headquartered in Boston and associated with the Congregational Church ministry.

Now, disassociated from the ministry, they operated the Oahu Charity School, a school intended to educate children of mixed racial backgrounds, many of them island children fathered by "white" sailors. For the most part, the school existed from contributions made by U.S. and British Navy men as well as men from the trading ships that visited the island. Wilson became so enthusiastic about the school that he talked with other traders along the California coast about it, and his influence was widely felt.(13)

In August, 1840, Thomas Larkin, an American trader and later United States consul at Monterey, wrote Johnstone, saying, "I send to you my eldest child, Oliver (he is seven years old April the 13th, 1841), for the purpose of putting him under your charge and schooling. Captain Wilson has informed me you have plenty of room for a few boys from this Coast, and we are anxious to have them sent to you...It will be unfortunate if it is otherwise, as there are six boys from eight to eleven years of age going to you by Captn. Paty's Barque...sons of Messrs. Spense, Watson, Kinloch, Wilson and Fitch."(14)

Romualdo and his brother spent the next five years of their young lives in the missionary school learning to read, write and speak English, all the while practicing traditional English manners. Apparently, they were free during

———————————— Page 30 please

EARLY 19th-century sailor's chapel located at Oahu. (Missionary Album, Sesquicentennial Edition.

SIDEBAR STORY 2

WAR WITH MEXICO IN CALIFORNIA

War between Mexico and the United States already appeared imminent in 1845 when John Charles Fremont, a noted military officer, mapmaker and explorer headed an expedition to California. Although his mission was ostensibly for mapmaking, Historian Allan Nevins suggests that Fremont received secret instructions for action in case a war between the two countries should break out.

Fremont was already at Sutter's Fort, now part of the city of Sacramento, when on Sunday, June 14, 1846, a party of American trappers and hunters from the Fort descended upon the Sonoma mission settlement in northern California and hung a handmade flag with a bear, a stripe, a star and the words, "California Republic" sewn upon it. History does not

provide any specific information clarifying Fremont's role in this event, but in early July he organized a California battalion of volunteers.

Meantime, United States Navy Commodore John Sloat waited in Pacific waters for word that the war with Mexico had actually started. Ten years earlier, Texas had declared itself a republic independent of Mexico. As a counter action in 1836, Santa Anna had attacked and killed the complete garrison of men station at Fort Alamo. Through the years afterward, Mexico refused to recognize Texas as an independent state.

In 1845, President James Polk sought an agreement with Mexico regarding the Rio Grande border and wanted to purchase California, but the Mexican government declined to negotiate. When Mexican and American patrols clashed along the border in April, 1846, Polk declared war. Word did not reach California until late June.

On July 7, 1846, Commodore Sloat came ashore at Monterey and raised the American flag. Two days later, the Navy did the same at Yerba Buena (later called San Francisco). Then, soon after, the Bear Flag at Sonoma was replaced with the stars and stripes.

When Commodore Sloat became gravely ill, he turned his command to Commodore Robert Stockton. Stockton soon brought Fremont's Volunteers under his command and appointed Fremont a major. Later, he asked Fremont to serve as military governor of California.

THE MEXICAN-AMERICAN WHO WON

JOHN FREMONT IN CALIFORNIA

After Los Angeles was occupied by a navy landing force and the California volunteers, Kit Carson was dispatched overland to inform authorities that the territory was secured for the United States. However, soon after this easy occupation of Los Angeles, the Mexican population rebelled against the enforcement of curfews and American military controls. Mexican Captain Maria Flores organized a revolt, forcing the small American contingent back to San Pedro.

Meantime, General Stephen Kearney had occupied New Mexico. Leaving a police force, he continued to California where he planned to organize a military and civil government. Kit Carson reached him and told him everything was under control in California. So, he did not anticipate any fighting upon arrival.

Kearney's men had marched 2000 miles overland, the longest movement of any military force in United States history. They arrived in California exhausted, half-starved and with horses replaced by mules and unbroken horses taken enroute.

ROMUALDO PACHECO'S CALIFORNIA

Camping near San Pascuel, Kearney's scouts discovered a small Mexican military contingent nearby. This group was under General Andres Pico, brother of the recently defeated Governor Pio Pico.

Kearney attacked the Mexican group, hoping to get fresh horses and rations. The Mexican military killed 22 American soldiers and injured many more, including Kearney himself.

Pico then withdrew and led his men north. Kearney and his men continued in the direction of Pueblo Los Angeles. On January 10, 1847, Kearney's force along with help from Commodore Stockton quelled the Los Angeles uprising.

Meantime, Fremont marched at the head of his volunteers from Sonoma and the bay area in the direction of Los Angeles, "conquering" every Mexican settlement along the coast of California, one at a time.

Fremont and his men celebrated Christmas in Santa Barbara before continuing to Cahuenga Canyon, the pass leading to Los Angeles. Here, Fremont's volunteers came face to face with General Andres Pico's group riding north after their engagement with General Kearney. Together, these leaders proceeded to the adobe house on the Cahuenga Rancho where they drew up the accords of the Treaty of Cahuenga, a document formally settling the war between the United States and the Mexicans in California.

When Fremont discovered that General Kearney had assumed the military governorship of California, he engaged his superior officer in a very serious quarrel. Fremont insisted that his appointment as military governor by Commodore Stockton took precedence.

Fremont's unwillingness to subordinate himself to General Kearney led to his arrest. Kearney brought a long list of charges against him. Fremont was taken to Washington D.C. for a military trial that led to his dismissal from the Army.

But Fremont remained a hero in the public's eyes. California's legislature elected him as one of its first two United States Senators in 1850. In 1856, he received the nomination for president of the United States by delegates of the new Republican Party. However, he was soundly defeated for office by James Buchanan.

*

THE MEXICAN-AMERICAN WHO WON

COMMODORE ROBERT STOCKTON

Romualdo Pacheco was fifteen years old when Commodore Robert Stockton took command as California's military governor in 1846. Romualdo was aboard one of his stepfather's trading ships at Monterey and again at San Francisco when their vessels were halted and searched by the U.S. Navy.

Stockton already had wide experience as a navy ship's officer when he arrived in California as commander of the Congress. He had seen action in the War of 1812 and the war against the Barbary Pirates in 1815. He took an active interest in the American Colonization Society, and in 1821, he was among those who journeyed to Africa to obtain the land that later became Liberia, the settlement area of many former American slaves who returned to the continent to establish a homeland.

Stockton resigned from the navy in 1850 and returned to New Jersey, the state of his birth. He served as a U.S. Senator for two years, then as president of the Delaware and Raritan Canal Company. The City of Stockton in California and an important downtown street in San Francisco are named for him. (Drawing from Annals of San Francisco)

CAPTAIN JOHN SUTTER

Romualdo Pacheco still attended the Oahu Charity School in the Sandwich Islands when John Sutter, a German-Swiss trader, passed through the Islands and then made his way to California.

Now, in Mexican territory, Sutter persuaded Mexican Governor Juan Bautista Alvarez to grant him eleven leagues of land in Northern California. There, he established a trading post between the Sacramento and American Rivers. It became known as Sutter's Fort, attracting American trappers and hunters. It later became the first stop for hundreds of overland settlers and gold seekers. (Drawing from Annals of San Francisco)

THE MEXICAN-AMERICAN WHO WON

MARIANO VALLEJO

Mariano Vallejo married Romualdo Pacheco's Aunt, Francisca Benicia Carrillo. As an officer in the Mexican military, he settled the lands north of San Francisco Bay for the Mexican government and served as commandante-general of California under his nephew, Mexican Governor Juan Bautista Alvarado.

THOMAS LARKIN

Like most Pacific Coast shipmasters, Romualdo Pacheco's stepfather, John Wilson, corresponded and traded with Thomas Larkin at Monterey. Larkin arrived in California in 1832. He soon established a general store and trading business. In 1843 and 1844, he served as United States Consul in California.

JACOB LEESE

Jacob Leese, a native of Ohio, bought a lot at Yerba Buena (later San Francisco), in 1836 and built the first solid structure on the sand dunes above the bay. The drawing below depicts a 4th of July celebration at his house during that same year. The next year, he built a large store on the beach. He married Rosalia, the sister of Mariano Vallejo.

THE MEXICAN-AMERICAN WHO WON

SAMUEL BRANNAN

Sam Brannon brought a Mormon group from the East coast to San Francisco by ship. He established San Francisco's first newspaper, The Star, and became California's first millionaire during the gold rush. In addition to his San Francisco interests, he later operated Brannon & Company in Sacramento, a large store catering to gold miners needs. (Drawing from Annals of San Francisco)

ROMUALDO PACHECO'S CALIFORNIA

from page 21

some summers and sailed back to Santa Barbara for long vacations.

In 1840, one of the years the boys attended the school, the Sandwich Islands missionary album reported 80 students under instruction.(15)(16)

By 1843, Romualdo and Mariano, now 12 and 13 years old, had returned to California. But their educations did not end. They were sent to sea on their stepfather's ships to learn navigation, accompanied by a tutor named Thomas B. Parker from Massachusetts. Parker would teach them geography, history, literature and other subjects providing a well-rounded education.(17)

These years were busy for Wilson and Scott's trading business, so the boys had ample opportunity to learn both navigation and the business operations of a trading company. Letters to Larkin tell us that Wilson traded in Valparaiso in 1843 and in the Sandwich Islands during part of 1844.(18)(19)

Wilson left the seafaring life after 1844, but Romualdo continued sailing with the Wilson-Scott fleet. During the years while their trading business prospered, Wilson and Scott purchased five ranchos in the area around Mission San Luis Obispo. When, in 1846, Governor Pio Pico began selling the mission buildings in California, the partners purchased the Mission San Luis Obispo buildings and gardens for the equivalent of $510 (20). They became the largest landowners in the area that would finally become San Luis Obispo County. Meanwhile, the size of the Wilson family grew. Wilson and Ramona had four more children, three girls and a son.

Romualdo experienced his first "official contacts" with the U. S. Navy July 7, 1846, aboard "the first of a fleet of three of his stepfather's vessels." This was the day Commodore John D. Sloat ordered the American flag raised at Monterey. Passing Monterey, the

Page 36 please

SAN LUIS OBISPO MISSION olive grove with crushing equipment. (Overland Monthly, Oct. 1871)

THE MEXICAN-AMERICAN WHO WON

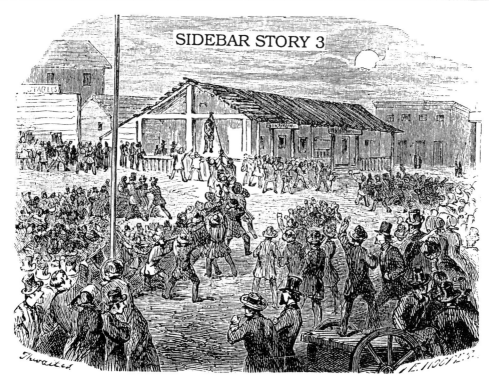

Hanging of Jenkins on the Plaza.

VIGILANTE JUSTICE

Much of California was almost lawless during the next two decades after the American occupation. During this restless and unsettled time, the people living in the state...hispanics, Chinese, Indians and anglos...all faced wanton crime of every description. Murder, robbery, gambling and incendiarism were frequent occurrences, even in the smallest settlements.

Racial intolerance made life difficult for those least able to defend themselves. Active bands of desperadoes, some of them seriously displaced persons, spread throughout the land. At the time, lawmen were few in number, poorly paid and generally helpless in the performance of their duties.

By the time California became a state in 1850, people already talked about the need for lynch laws, and by June, 1851, a "Vigilance Committee" took form in San Francisco. On June 11, the Committee hanged a man on the plaza for stealing. Lynchings were soon a common means of resolving criminal acts. Although this Committee dissipated within a year, its effect remained a constant reminder of what could happen when crime became rampant.

ROMUALDO PACHECO'S CALIFORNIA

In August, 1856, James King, editor of the San Francisco Evening Bulletin, was murdered by James P. Casey, editor of the Sunday Times. At the time, Casey was an aspirant for state political office. He had served time in Sing Sing, the New York State Prison before coming to California. King revealed Casey's background in the Bulletin and charged him with fraudulently seeking office.

A new vigilante committee tried Casey and another murderer, finding both of them guilty. The Committee hanged them in the open street in front of the Vigilance Committee's new office.

But San Francisco was not the only place in early California where Vigilante Committees organized to stop crime. In 1858, weary of lawlessness, San Luis Obispo County citizens formed a group that tried and hung several murderers and bandits.

Romualdo Pacheco, shortly after being elected a state senator, led a group of deputized Californios in pursuit of two bandits. His riders brought one of them back to San Luis Obispo for hanging.

Hanging of Whittaker and McKenzie.

The California Star. 1847

Regular Mail.

Our readers will be pleased to learn, that Gov. KEARNY has established a semi-monthly mail, to run regularly between San Francisco and San Diego. This mail is to be carried on horseback, by a party consisting of two soldiers; and is to commence on the 19th inst. Starting every other Monday from San Diego, and San Francisco, the parties to meet at Captain Dana's Ranch, the next Sunday to exchange Mails; start back on their respective routes the next morning, and arrive at San Diego and San Francisco, on the Sunday following, and so continuing. The mail will thus be carried once a fortnight from San Diego to San Francisco, and from San Francisco to San Diego.

From San Diego the Mail will arrive at San Luis Rey, Monday evening; at the Pueblo de los Angeles, Wednesday noon; at Santa Barbara, Friday evening; at Capt. Dana's Ranch, Sunday evening; at Monterey, Thursday evening; at San Francisco, Sunday evening.

From San Francisco, the Mail will arrive at Monterey, Wednesday evening; at Capt. Dana's Ranch, Sunday evening; at Santa Barbara, Tuesday evening; at the Pueblo de los Angeles, Friday noon; at San Luis Rey, Saturday evening; at San Diego, Sunday evening. Letters and papers carried free of expense.

SIDEBAR STORY 4

THE DONNER PARTY

Ninety men, women and children left Independence, Missouri in a wagon train headed west during the summer of 1846. Enroute, they met other groups who joined them. The train finally included two or perhaps three hundred wagons stretching for two miles along the trail.

They moved across the great plains, around the most difficult part of the Rockies and past Salt Lake. But quarrels and bickering throughout the trip slowed their progress. Some people wanted to go one way and others another.

In an encounter with Indians some members of the party lost their oxen and horses. They had to ride in the wagons of others, and in some cases, walk. It was mid-October by the time the expedition reached the Sierra-Nevada Mountains.

Supplies were already reduced to bare subsistence as they began their climb. Then snow fell even earlier than usual. Constant storms finally blocked all progress. They became scattered into small groups along the snow-covered mountain trail, losing track of one another for days at a time. Families made shelters of whatever they could find. When food supplies were exhausted, they boiled cowhides and tried to eat them. Weaker members of the party became ill. Many died. Those who lived became more and more desperate, eating the flesh of the dead.

These sample entries in one party members diary published in 1847 reveal part of this tragic experience:

"Dec.21, Millon got back last night from Donner's camp, sad news, Jacob Donner, Sam'l Shoemaker, Rhinehart and Smith are dead...snowed all night with a strong wind."

"Jan. 17, Eliza Williams came here this morning, Lanthron crazy last night, provisions scarce, hides are main substance...may the Almighty send us help."

"Feb. 25, Mrs. Murphy says the wolves are about to dig up the dead bodies around her shanty, but the nights are too cold to watch them..."

"Feb. 26, the Donners told the California folks four days ago that they would commence on the dead people...if they did not find their cattle..."

"Mar. 1, Ten men arrived this morning from Bear Valley with provisions...we are to leave (for Sutter's Fort) in 2 or 3 days..."

The California Star.

Names of the late Emigration from the U. S., who were prevented by the Snow from crossing the California Mountains, Oct. 31st, 1846.

ARRIVED IN CALIFORNIA.

William Graves,	Simon Murphy,
Sarah Fosdick,	Mary Murphy,
Mary Graves,	Harriet Pike,
Ellen Graves,	Miomin Pike,
Viney Graves,	Wm. Eddy,
Nancy Graves,	Patrick Breen,
Jonathan Graves,	Margaret Breen,
Elizabeth Graves,	John Breen,
Loithy Donner,	Edward Breen,
Lean Donner,	Patrick Breen, Jr.
Francis Donner,	Simon Breen.
Georgeana Donner,	James Breen,
Eliza Donner,	Peter Breen.
John Battiste,	Isabella Breen,
Solomon Hook.	Eliza Williams,
Geo. Donner, Jun.	James F. Reed,
Mary Donner,	Mrs. Reed,
Mrs. Woolfinger,	Virginia Reed,
Lewis Kiesburg,	Martha Reed,
Mrs Kiesburg,	James Reed,
William Foster,	Thomas Reed,
Sarah Foster,	Noah James.

PERISHED IN THE MOUNTAINS.

C. T. STANTON.	Bertha Kiesburg, (child)
Mr. Graves,	Lewis Kiesburg,
Mrs. Graves,	Mrs. Murphy,
Mr. J. Fosdick,	Lemuel Murphy,
Franklin Graves,	George Foster,
John Denton,	Catherine Pike,
Geo. Donner, Sen.	Ellen Eddy,
Mrs. Donner,	Margurette Eddy,
Charles Berger,	James Eddy,
Joseph Rhinehart,	Patrick Dolan,
Jacob Donner,	Augustus Spitzer,
Betsey Donner,	Milton Elliot,
Wm. Johnson,	Lantron Murphy,
Isaac Donner,	
Lewis Donner,	Mr. Pike.
Samuel Donner,	Antonio, [New Mexican]
Samuel Shoemaker,	Lewis, (Sutter's Indian)
James Smith,	Salvadore, do do
Balis Williams,	

Emigrants in the Mountains.

It is probably not generally known to the people, that there is now in the California mountains in a most distressing situation, a party of emigrants from the United States, who were prevented from crossing the mountains by an early heavy fall of snow. The party consists of about sixty persons, men, women and children. They were, almost entirely out of provisions, when they reached the foot of the mountain, and but for the timely succor afforded them by Capt. J. A. Sutter, one of the most humane and liberal men in California, they must have all perished in a few days. Captain Sutter as soon as he ascertained their situation, sent five mules loaded with provisions to them. A second party was dispatched with provisions for them, but they found the mountain impassable, in consequence of the snow. We hope that our citizens will do something for the relief of these unfortunate people.

THE MEXICAN-AMERICAN WHO WON

from page 30

Wilson-Scott vessels were stopped by the U. S. Sloop of War, The Cyane, and informed "that Mexico and the United States were now at War." Their vessels were searched and then permitted to continue. A few days later it happened again as their ships entered San Francisco Bay.(21)

The occupation of California by the Americans opened new challenges for young Romualdo and his brother, Mariano. In every way, both their educations and their hispanic-anglo family backgrounds prepared them for the mixed new population that would make up California.

Their competence in reading, writing and speaking the English language gave them an extraordinary head start in the new California. Under the Treaty of Guadaloupe, all residents of California were now citizens of the United States unless they chose to the contrary.

By 1853, Romualdo assumed major financial responsi bilities on behalf of his stepfather. Here is an example of a business letter he sent to Abel Stearns, a trader in San Pedro:

"Mr. Stearns, Sir, I have much pleasure in forwarding you the amt. of your a/c $4160 (four thousand one hundred and sixty dollars) with many thanks for your kindness. I should have sent it before had I had an opportunity but such has not been the case. My father desires me to present you his best respects and receive the same from Yours, Romualdo Pacheco." Stearns marked this letter "Rec'd July 23, 1853."(22) Romualdo was now 22 years old, and he had met every challenge well. It would soon be time for his next important move.

Preparing For Public Office

In hindsight, Romualdo's entire life appears like a quiet

=Page 39 please

Dissolution of Copartnership.

The Copartnership, heretofore existing under the firm of SCOTT & WILSON, has this day been dissolved by mutual consent. All persons having accounts with the said firm, are requested to present them. And those icdebted to the same, are hereby informed, that their accounts must be paid, and cancelled before EIGHT MONTHS; or they will be handed over to their Attorney at law for recovery.

JAMES SCOTT.
JOHN WILSON.

Yerba Buena, Jan'y 22d. 1847.

Aviso al Publico.

Habiendose desuelta mutuamente hoy dia la compania conocida bajo el nombre de SCOTT y WILSON. Se suplica a toda persona que tenga cuentas con ellos a prosentarlos inmediamentamente. Y los que adeudan se sirviran de pagar y cubrir sus compromisas, antes del termino de OCHO MESES; de lo contrario, se pasara la cuentaa un Procurador para su cobro.

JAIME SCOTT.
JUAN WILSON.

Yerba Buena, y Enero 22 de 1847.   3 3t

JOHN WILSON-JAMES SCOTT PARTNERSHIP DISSOLVED

John Wilson, Romualdo Pacheco's stepfather, and James Scott, his longtime partner, placed this notice in the San Francisco Star January 22, 1847 informing the public that their 20-year partnership was ended. Both came from England. Scott died in 1850, leaving his large California estate to his sisters and mother.

THE MEXICAN-AMERICAN WHO WON

SIDEBAR STORY 5

1849 CALIFORNIA GOLD RUSH

When James Wilson Marshall, a master carpenter, rode into the foothills to a place called Coloma (beautiful vale) on the south fork of the American River, the world soon had reason to take note.

Marshall had contracted with John Sutter to build a sawmill at water's edge. One day in January, 1848, while deepening the tailrace and clearing the water of obstructions, Marshall caught a glimpse of a glittering particle behind a riffle of stone.

The news of Marshall's find leaked surprisingly slowly, and, at first, attracted little attention. There had been idle rumors about gold in California from the time of its discovery. In March, 1848, a news item about Marshall's find appeared in the Californian and the California Star, scarcely arousing anyone. But later, this story appeared in the Star:

"Saturday, June 10, 1848- It is quite unnecessary to remind our readers of the prospects of California at this time, as the effect of this gold-washing enthusiasm...is unmistakably apparent.

ARGONAUTS ALONG SAN FRANCISCO BAY make ready to journey to the mining country. The diggings took them from Coloma, about 45 miles northeast of Fort Sutter to Mariposa in the foothills of the Sierras farther south.

ROMUALDO PACHECO'S CALIFORNIA

AT FIRST, THE '49ERS USED THE HAND-ROCKING MOTION of pans to separate gold dust from sand and silt. Then came the long box with cradle rockers. The rocker made it possible to process a great deal more sand, but it usually required three miners working together...one shoveling dirt, another pouring buckets of water into the box to wash the sand down the trough and a third rocking the cradle.

"Every seaport as far south as San Diego and every interior town and nearly every rancho from the base of the mountain in which the gold has been found...to the Mission of San Luis, south, has become suddenly drained of human beings."

This issue of Sam Brannon's newspaper was sent abroad. The newspaper office itself was soon closed so employees could pan for gold. By 1852, the peak year of the gold rush, about 100,000 miners from around the world brought in $80 million in gold. This event changed California forever.

The rush was made easier because two years earlier Congress had granted subsidies to two new merchant steamer lines, the United States Mail Steamship Company sailing between New York and Chagres on the Atlantic side of the Panama Isthmus and the Pacific Mail Steamship Company making the voyage from Panama to California and Oregon.

THE MEXICAN-AMERICAN WHO WON

> Treasurers Office
> County of San Luis Obispo
> October 28, 1850
>
> Received by the hand of Henry A Tefft for Francisco Branch the sum of $1430.65 being the full amount of his State & County Tax for the Year 1860 on his real & personal property to this County
>
> Jean Wilson
> Treasurer
> by
> Freeman
> Deputy Treasurer

DURING THE time that Romualdo Pacheco's stepfather, John Wilson, served as treasurer of San Luis Obispo County, a deputy carrried out operational details for him. This receipt identifies Henry Tefft, son-in-law of William Goodwin Dana, grantee of the Nipomo Rancho.

from page 36

preparation for public life, and his family provided him many models.

His cousin in Santa Barbara, Pablo de la Guerra, had been alcalde (mayor) in that pueblo toward the end of the Mexican period and represented his district at the California Constitutional Convention in the new American period. He also served as a state senator for the San Luis Obispo-Santa Barbara district in 1853.(23)(24)

His Uncle Mariano Vallejo, married to Francisca Benicia Carrillo, his mother's sister, represented the Sonoma district in almost every public way. During the Mexican period he served as commandante-general under his nephew, Governor Juan Bautista Alvarado. In the new American era, he attended the Constitutional Convention on behalf of his district and became the first state senator from the Sonoma area. The City of Vallejo was named for him, and the City of Benicia was named for his wife, Romualdo's aunt.(25)

As the towns and counties of California organized their governments in 1850, Romualdo saw his stepfather elected treasurer of San Luis Obispo County (26). Then, the next year, his brother, Mariano, ran for and was elected state assemblyman from the district (27). He was elected again in 1852, but resigned.

In one way or another, Mariano represented the family's land interests for the rest of his life, eventually owning the Piedra Blancas land grant, the nucleus of the present-day ranch owned by the

39

ROMUALDO PACHECO'S CALIFORNIA

Hearst Corporation. The public is most aware of this area along Highway One because of the location of Hearst Castle, given to the state in 1958.

In May, 1852, the state legislature provided for the election of a board of supervisors in each county, and John Wilson was elected to the first board. That same year, Romualdo's cousin, Joaquin Carrillo in Santa Barbara, who earlier had been appointed to complete an unfulfilled term as district judge for San Luis Obispo, Buenaventura and Santa Barbara counties, was now elected to this position (28). Altogether, Joaquin Carrillo would serve as district judge for the next twelve years.

****
County Judge
Romualdo Pacheco

Soon after Romualdo became 22 years old, he, too, made a bid for public office. The year was 1853. He ran for and was elected county judge (29). It was not a fulltime position during those years. The San Luis Obispo County Court Index does not show many cases during this four-year period, but then the whole population of the county remained less than 1000 people. Most of Romualdo's time was probably devoted to the family's ranchos while he gained some reputation and experience as a public official.

Judge Pacheco could conduct court sessions in either English or Spanish, depending upon the needs of San Luis Obispo County complainants and defendents. He handled a number of cases in which people sought recovery of money or property which they thought rightfully belonged to them. Among them, he called his own stepfather on November 8, 1854 to answer charges of holding property

Page 42 please

ROMUALDO PACHECO organized a party of Californios with good horses, leading them in fast pursuit of two robbers and thieves who escaped the San Luis Obispo vigilantes. They did not stop until they reached Pueblo de Los Angeles where they captured Nieves Robles and brought him back for hanging.

THE MEXICAN-AMERICAN WHO WON

MISSION OF SAN LUIS OBISPO.

THE EARLY MISSION settlement of San Luis Obispo. Left, the French Hotel and Restaurant. Right, Mission San Luis Obispo dating from 1772. In 1846, Mexican Governor Pio Pico sold this mission to John Wilson, James Scott and James McKinley for $510. In 1859, the United States Land Commission returned ownership to Bishop Joseph S. Alemany of the Catholic Church. (Overland Monthly, Oct. 1871)

ROMUALDO PACHECO'S CALIFORNIA

from page 40

allegedly belonging to a man named Joseph Levey. The court record shows that Wilson responded by saying, "I have no property belonging to Levey. Levey has been my servant a long time, and we have a great many dealings between us. He owes me three thousand seven hundred dollars." Others testified on Wilson's behalf, and the young judge decided the case in his stepfather's favor.(30)

California State Senator Pacheco

When Romualdo Pacheco received word in 1857 that his cousin, Pablo, was not running for state senator in the district, he sought the office for himself. His opponent was a man named Dr. S. B. Brinkerhoff, a well-known citizen of Santa Barbara. In these two counties, the Mexican population still remained in the majority. When the balloting was over, Pacheco, now 26 years old, had been elected. (31)

The Vigilantes

During the period after the American takeover, Central California was practically lawless. Many Mexican men could not find a place in the new social system, and some unscrupulous Americans took advantage of the ineffective operation of the law during the transition.

The Americans in the San Luis Obispo-Santa Barbara district soon called upon their new Senator

ROMUALDO PACHECO'S FAMILY PROPERTY- This recent sketch was taken from a photograph of the two-story adobe casa located on the Pecho y Islay land grant in San Luis Obispo County. John Wilson and his partner, James Scott, acquired the grant from Francisco Padilla.

ROMUALDO PACHECO'S CALIFORNIA

ROMUALDO PACHECO'S FAMILY PROPERTY- This is a recent drawing taken from a photo of the casa located on the Canada de Los Osos Rancho in San Luis Obispo County. The communities of Los Osos and Baywood developed on this land.

Pacheco to use his influence among the Californios to help fight the rampant crime that continued to grow worse.(32)

"Scarcely three months have passed without the discovery at some point or another within 40 miles of here of one to three skeletons or corpses," a local lawyer and journalist named Walter Murray wrote in a letter dated May 28, 1858 to his sister in England. In this letter, he described the whole episode of crime in the area leading to his role in forming a Vigilance Committee.(33)

About this time, crime struck closer to home for Senator Pacheco. On June 10, 1858 one of the herdsmen on the Canada de Los Osos, his family's home rancho, reported seeing Huero Rafael Herrado, a desperado who rode with gang leader Pio Linares. John Wilson quickly sent word to the San Luis Obispo settlement, and within a day men began arriving from all over the county determined to capture this ruffian and any others riding with him.

Before these men finished their work, Pio Linares was killed in an ambush on the rancho, and other members of his gang were captured and hanged in the plaza at San Luis Obispo.(34)

Page 48 please

ROMUALDO PACHECO'S CALIFORNIA

SIDEBAR STORY 6
CALIFORNIA'S INDIANS

During Romualdo Pacheco's early life, there were still many Indians living in California. Many of them lived in or near the mission compounds or on ranchos operated by the missionaries. Others ran free in tribal groups in northern California and in the inland valley. Modern books and museum dioramas tend to describe Indian culture by the way tribes dressed, by their crafts and by their hunting and fishing paraphenalia. Shell mounds and old camp sites help interprete food preferences. Rock paintings, basket decoration and other art lead to speculation about religion and abstract thought.

Not enough is written about their treatment by the Spanish and Mexican soldiers assigned to the missions nor about the semi-slavery state in which they were held as "christians" at the missions. Nor about their efforts to defend themselves or break free from the European intrusion upon their lives.

THE MEXICAN-AMERICAN WHO WON

Thousands of Indians, particularly those living inland, away from the missions, remained free. Many others who had fallen under the domination of priests and soldiers resented what happened to them. If they failed to obey orders, they were whipped. If they ran away, they were tracked and brought back to the mission compound. It is little wonder that their resentment showed itself in so many cases of arson, stealing, revolt and killing.

The first major tragedy occurred at Mission San Diego during the night of November 4, 1775 when several hundred Indians from local tribal groups stormed the mission bent upon its destruction. They burned it to the ground and drove a dozen arrows into the body of Padre Luis Jayme. Presidio soldiers three leagues away didn't even know about this onslaught until the next morning.

In 1780 the Spanish tried to establish two missions along the Colorado River, but in July 1781, the Yuma Indians, led by Chief Palma, slaughtered nearly all of the men involved...priests, soldiers and settlers. Interestingly, the Indians showed a certain civility by sparing the women and children. The Spanish were forced to permanently set aside establishment of these missions.

When Governor Pablo Vicente de Sola first tried to establish settlements north of San Francisco Bay in 1816, the Modoc Indians attacked the soldiers who rode into their territory and turned them back to their reed rafts in the bay. There were several efforts to take this territory by the Spanish, but the Indians continued to fight off occupation.

Perhaps the most far-reaching Indian revolt began at Mission Santa Ines in 1824. After a visiting Chumash Indian from Mission La Purisima was beaten by a soldier of the guard, a group of Indians attacked the mission that night with burning stakes. They set fire not only to the mission but to the outbuildings. They returned to Purisima, took the soldiers and priests captive and used the mission walls as a fort against a contingent of soldiers from both Monterey and Santa Barbara.

When word reached the Indians at Santa Barbara Mission, they, too, revolted. Eventually, all of these attacks were quelled, but not without the loss of lives. Indian dissatisfaction reverberated up and down the El Camino Real.

Romualdo Pacheco's uncle, Mariano Vallejo, fought numerous battles against the Indians in Northern California.

ROMUALDO PACHECO'S CALIFORNIA

Even after American occupation of California, Indians continued their rampages against the settlements. An article in the The Star in 1847 said, "It is to be regretted that nothing effective can be done to prevent the alarming encroachments of the horse-thief Indians." These raids upon the rancheros occurred all along the coast.

"From the Tularies downwards, to even the Port of San Diego, this growing evil is still seriously prevalent," The Star reported. "Emboldened by success, they are daily becoming more and more desperate and cases of murder and numerous attempts at life are fresh in the memories of us all."

The newspaper spoke of Romualdo Pacheco's home community. "At the Mission of San Luis Obispo the residents are in continued alarm and not a week ago the Indians came down upon them, drove away their few remaining horses."

In a letter dated June 6, 1847 to Governor Richard Mason, William Goodwin Dana, grantee of the Nipomo Rancho near San Luis Obispo, wrote, "A military force is absolutely necessary to this place. The wild Indians are committing raids and carrying off droves of horses. If some prompt measures are not adopted, the farmers will have to abandon the ranchos. Horrid murders are reported by the alcalde."

California Indians did not give up their place without a valiant struggle. Many of them integrated with the Mexicans, and many died of white men's diseases. But there are still a few descendents in places like the Santa Ines Reservation.

THE MEXICAN-AMERICAN WHO WON

CALIFORNIA INDIANS AS DEPICTED BY AN ARTIST ON THE STAFF OF HARPER's NEW MONTHLY MAGAZINE IN 1872.

NATIVE OF CALIFORNIA.

ROMUALDO PACHECO'S CALIFORNIA

from page 43

But Herrada and Nieves Robles escaped capture. Senator Pacheco received word that Herrada had bought or traded for a horse with a Mexican at Pio Linare's ranchito and headed south. He organized a party of Californios with good horses. He then arranged for Sheriff Francisco Castro to deputize them so their actions would be legal. He led a fast chase in pursuit of these robbers and thieves that took his riders to Santa Barbara. Here, the sheriff and five other men joined him in the pursuit.

On Friday, June 18, Senator Pacheco rode through Cahuenga Pass where his father had been killed 26 years earlier. The trail ended in Los Angeles. They did not capture Herrada, but they brought back Nieves Robles. This desperado, too, was tried and hung by the Vigilance Committee in the San Luis Obispo plaza. The Senator and his riders enjoyed a special respect among the Americanos, and Pacheco's career as a state politician was now well-launched.(35)

****

1859-Romualdo Pacheco Goes to England

Richard Henry Dana returned to the California coast in 1859 to review old times and places of his seafaring days in 1835-36. He took passage aboard the Steamer Senator, and on Saturday, August 20, 1859, he wrote: "Among the passengers I noticed an elderly gentleman, thin, with sandy hair and a face that seemed familiar. He took off his glove and showed one shriveled hand. I went to him and said, "Captain Wilson, I believe." (36) Once again, John Wilson became a reference for Dana, this time as sequel to his earlier book. Dana's

Page 50 please

A vaquero with whip herds Spanish cattle into corral. (Scribner's Monthly, 1878 Volume)

THE MEXICAN-AMERICAN WHO WON

MONTEREY PUEBLO served as seat of government for Alta California during much of the Spanish-Mexican period. Thomas Larkin, United States Consul during late Mexican rule, contracted with the Mexican government for the construction of the two-story adobe custom house shown at right in top early engraving. (Annals of San Francisco, 1854)

San Carlos Borromeo de Carmelo Mission at Carmel was headquarters for Padre Junipero Serra, founder of the California Mission system beginning in 1769. (Annals of San Francisco)

ROMUALDO PACHECO'S CALIFORNIA

from page 48

work added much to Wilson's fame along the coast.

Romualdo Pacheco did not run for state senator in 1859. Instead, his cousin, Pablo de la Guerra was again elected to this position. During his term, Guerra was also elected president-protem of the Senate, then president and finally lieutenant governor after Governor Milton Lathan resigned and Lieutenant Governor John Downey moved into the governor's chair.(37) This action represented quite an achievement for the Californios and a great compliment to Guerra. No Mexican had reached this position in California government since the American takeover.

Pacheco found himself deeply engrossed in serious family problems. His stepfather's health was failing. In February, 1860, John Wilson called local friends Charles H. Johnson, Walter Murray, William Borland and W. I. Graves to the family townhouse next to the mission in order that they might witness his signature to a last will and testament.

In addition to Romualdo and Mariano, he wanted to remember all of his children: his daughters..Maria Ignacia, Ramona and Juana; and his son, John, the youngest and apparently the apple of his eye.

While his own son, John, was very young, Wilson sent him to his family in England to be educated, and the boy remained there. The most important of the family ranchos, the Canada de los Osos, the home rancho, would go to young John upon Wilson's death. The boy would also share in the balance of the estate.(38)

Now, free of public office and undoubtedly concerned about the future of the family holdings, Romualdo Pacheco boarded a ship on the Pacific Coast and began the long journey to Liverpool, England where his half-brother lived. During his stay, he also traveled to London several times where he visited the family of his San Luis Obispo friends, Walter and Alexander Murray. In an undated letter from his friends' mother to Alexander Murray, probably written in October or November, 1860, we get some impressions about 29-year-old Pacheco at this state of his life.

She wrote: "We have been much pleased with an introduction to the Hon. R. Pacheco. He is indeed a handsome, polished gentleman, such a one as I could scarcely have thought California would have produced. He is very agreeable. He is to dine with us, also Uncle Hopwood soon." (39)

During Pacheco's absence from the United States, the Republican party continued to grow in importance, and in November, 1860, Abraham Lincoln was elected president. Then, in April, 1861, southern rebels fired on Fort Sumter, and the Civil War began.

We do not know what understanding Pacheco may have reached with his half-brother and the boy's English relatives, but young John never returned to California.

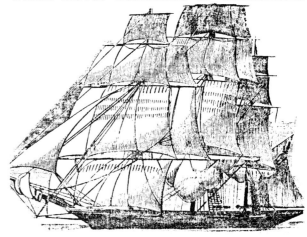

50

THE MEXICAN-AMERICAN WHO WON

Even as late as 1891, testimony in settling the estate indicates that he remained in Liverpool.(40)

Civil War Politics

When Pacheco returned home, he found the new Republican Party enjoying immense popularity, and he cast his lot with them. In the balloting held September 4, 1861, he was again elected state senator from his district. Unfortunately, his victory was almost immediately marred by family tragedy.

John Wilson Dies

State Senator Pacheco's stepfather died in October, 1861. This intense and driven Scotsman who had risked his life a thousand times on the high seas in his small trading vessels, grown wealthy on both land and sea, and reared a family 7000 miles from his birthplace, died in his bed at home.

Born a Scotsman and a protestant, he had married a Mexican-California woman and become a catholic and citizen of Mexico. He died as a naturalized American and was laid to rest in a small catholic cemetery in San Luis Obispo under a high tombstone that still stands, a reminder of the boldness and courage of anglo seamen along the California coast and throughout the Pacific Ocean in the early nineteenth century. Romualdo Pacheco and his brother were named joint executors of the estate, and they called upon their longstanding friend, Walter Murray,

Page 60 please

Golden Gate and Fort Point

EARLY YERBA BUENA, later San Francisco- Entrance to San Francisco Bay, known as the Golden Gate, with Fort Point as its protector. The location of this American fort above the bay was also site of the earlier presidio for the Spanish and Mexican governments. (Annals of San Francisco, 1854)

THE MEXICAN-AMERICAN WHO WON

MISSION DOLORES

MISSION San Francisco de Asis, popularly known as Mission Dolores, as it appeared in 1854 with priest of an earlier period. (Annals of San Francisco, 1854)

YERBA BUENA

YERBA BUENA Cove, 1849-50, where hundreds of ships found their way loaded with men hoping to find gold. (Annals of San Francisco, 1854)

LOOKING NORTH along Montgomery Street from California Street in San Francisco, 1849-50. (Annals of San Francisco, 1854)

THE MEXICAN-AMERICAN WHO WON

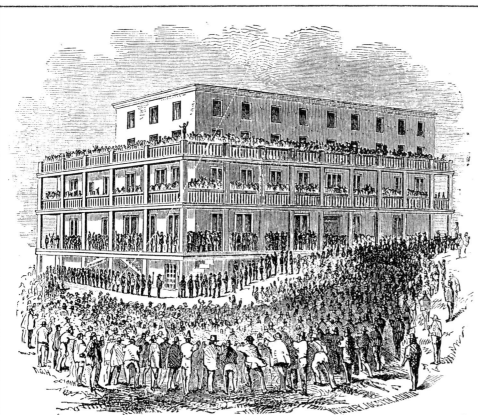

SAN FRANCISCO'S CITY HALL- Grand opening February 22, 1851. (Annals of San Francisco, 1854)

SAN FRANCISCO FIRE-May 4, 1851. The City had also experienced a major fire in May, 1850. The wooden structures of the day were prone to fire and fire equipment was at a minimum. (Annals of San Francisco, 1854)

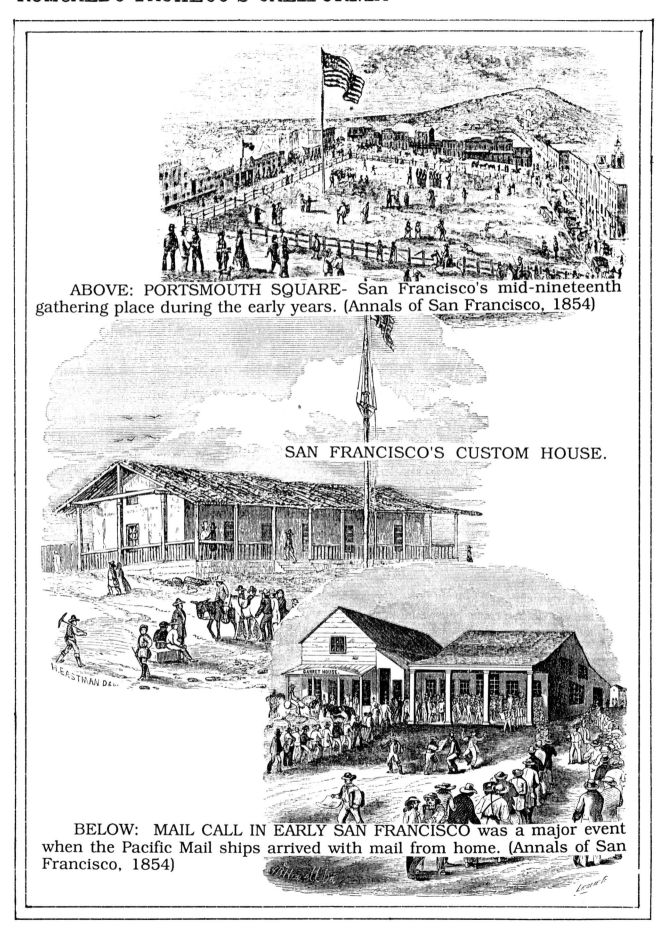

ABOVE: PORTSMOUTH SQUARE- San Francisco's mid-nineteenth gathering place during the early years. (Annals of San Francisco, 1854)

SAN FRANCISCO'S CUSTOM HOUSE.

BELOW: MAIL CALL IN EARLY SAN FRANCISCO was a major event when the Pacific Mail ships arrived with mail from home. (Annals of San Francisco, 1854)

THE MEXICAN-AMERICAN WHO WON

FIGHTING MUD, RATS AND OTHER UNSEEMLY CONDITIONS during the rainy season in San Francisco. (Annals of San Francisco, 1854)

"GREASERS, COOLIES AND NIGGERS," the Annals of San Francisco called the Mexicans, Chinese and Blacks who came looking for gold. Soon after this time, Romualdo Pacheco ran for county judge in San Luis Obispo and was elected by the largely Mexican population. (Annals of San Francisco, 1854)

1854- SATURDAY NIGHT at the California Exchange, San Francisco. (Annals of San Francisco, 1854)

MID-19TH CENTURY CALIFORNIA FASHION PLATE showing oriental, hispanic, anglo and black women of San Francisco. (Annals of San Francisco, 1854)

WINN'S BRANCH EXTENSION, an elegant mid-19th century restaurant in San Francisco. (Annals of San Francisco, 1854)

THE EL DORADO- A San Francisco saloon and gambling place during the 1850's. (Annals of San Francisco, 1854)

ROMUALDO PACHECO'S CALIFORNIA

from page 51

an attorney, to handle legal matters associated with the settlement.(41)

General Romualdo Pacheco

Relieved of direct responsibility for the ranchos by family and lawyer, Romualdo turned almost completely to a life of politics. The year 1863 became the most far-reaching and most rewarding time of his career. But it must also have been wearing. While the Civil War raged, his popularity reached new heights, and the demand for his services could not have been greater.

The state government quickly discovered that many Californios would fight for their adopted country, and so the government encouraged the forming of a cavalry battalion made up entirely of men of Mexican descent. To help accomplish this purpose, Governor Leland Stanford appointed Senator Pacheco a brigadier general in the state militia (42). If anyone among the Californios enjoyed the respect necessary to organize a battalion, certainly Pacheco did.

Salvador Vallejo, who had been a tough and reckless officer under his brother, Mariano Vallejo (Romualdo Pacheco's uncle), during the Mexican period, joined Pacheco as a commissioned officer. They also called upon Jose Ramon Pico, a former officer in the Mexican Army and distant cousin of Pacheco's mother, to accept a commission and

Page 63 please

ST. MARY'S CATHEDRAL

ROMUALDO PACHECO MARRIED Mary Catherine McIntire October 31, 1863 on his thirty-second birthday at St. Mary's Cathedral in San Francisco. He had just been elected treasurer of California. (Annals of San Francisco, 1854)

THIS NINETEENTH CENTURY BRIDE looks very much as Mary McIntire Pacheco may have appeared on her wedding day. (Peterson's Magazine, 1882 Volume)

CALIFORNIA STEAM NAVIGATION COMPANY.

Organized March 1st, 1854. - - - Capital Stock, $2,500,000.

The following are the Officers for the Years 1869-70.

President, B. M. HARTSHORNE; Vice President, W. H. TAYLOR; Secretary, S. O. PUTNAM; Trustees, B. M. HARTSHORNE, W. H. TAYLOR, A. HAYWARD, W. C. RALSTON, WM. ALVORD, A. REDINGTON, LLOYD TEVIS, JOHN BENSLEY and S. F. BUTTERWORTH. Agents —Sacramento, ALFRED REDINGTON; Marysville, C. H. KIMBALL; Red Bluff, SAMUEL JAYNES; Stockton, T. C. WALKER.

Departure from Broadway Wharf,
CARRYING THE UNITED STATES MAILS.

Steamer CAPITAL	Capt. E. A. POOLE.
Steamer YOSEMITE	Capt. E. A. POOLE.
Steamer CHRYSOPOLIS	Capt. A. FOSTER.
Steamer ANTELOPE	Capt. CHARLES THORNE.
Steamer JULIA	Capt. W. BROMLEY.
Steamer AMADOR	Capt. JOHN FOURATT.

ONE OF THE ABOVE STEAMERS WILL
Leave every day, at four o'clock, P.M.
(SUNDAYS EXCEPTED) FOR
SACRAMENTO and STOCKTON,
Connecting with the Light-Draught Steamers for
MARYSVILLE, COLUSA AND RED BLUFF.

For further particulars, apply at the OFFICE OF THE COMPANY,
N.E. Cor. Jackson and Front Sts., San Francisco.
B. M. HARTSHORNE, President.

THE MEXICAN-AMERICAN WHO WON

THE ARRIVAL AND DEPARTURE OF SHIPS in San Francisco created a great deal of excitement during the mid-19th century. Romualdo Pacheco sailed frequently along the Pacific Coast and on the Sacramento River to the capitol to and from his home in Central California. (Annals of San Francisco, 1854)

from page 60

help recruit men to fill one of the cavalry companies. Organizing the battalion was partly a family affair in the beginning. Captains Vallejo and Pico both had the necessary experience from their days in the Mexican military in California.

The Californios, the state's finest riders, quickly came together as a unit expecting to go east and enter battle, but their assignment took them no farther than Yuma, Arizona where they served as border guards with specific orders to prevent the movement of arms from California that might reach southern rebels.(43)

In politics, the war led to a coalition between the Union Democrats, referred to as the "short hairs", and the Republicans, known as the "long hairs". In this union of parties, there were actually more Democrats than Republicans at the 1863 joint party convention in Sacramento. As a military man sworn to uphold the Union, General Romualdo Pacheco found himself swept into allegiance with the Union Democrats, and he became the party's nominee for state treasurer. The party chose F. F. Low as its candidate for governor.

Vigorous support of the Union and Abraham Lincoln became the focus of all state political candidates hoping to get elected. Again, Pacheco's military role proved his position as a patriotic American. Along with all of the candidates under the coalition banner, he was elected to his first statewide

Page 65 please

THE MEXICAN-AMERICAN WHO WON

from page 63

office.(44)

Romualdo Pacheco Meets Mary McIntire

But his election to statewide office and his military duties were only part of what crowded his thoughts at the time. Someone special had entered his life. He had been courting a young woman named Mary Catherine McIntire, a talented and obviously creative playwright. Without question, she drew him even deeper into the social-cultural context of American thought. She was slim-faced, very fair-complexioned and clearly had the social graces so important to Pacheco's political life.

Miss McIntire was eleven years younger than State Treasurer Pacheco. A few years earlier, she had arrived in California with her mother and two younger sisters from Danville, Kentucky.

She and Pacheco exchanged vows October 31, 1863, his thirty-second birthday, in a small chapel at St. Mary's Cathedral in San Francisco.

In the years ahead, Mary Pacheco would write a number of stage plays, most of them produced in San Francisco. Her talent and his

Page 68 please

PUEBLO DE LOS ANGELES

Utilizing early plats showing the first layout of Los Angeles around a plaza in 1781, the late Santa Barbara artist Russell Ruiz provided this sketch for the Conference of California Historical Societies program in 1981. Historical societies from all over California gathered in celebration of the city's bicentennial.

SIDEBAR STORY 7

THE BIRTH OF LOS ANGELES

They came from the poorest classes of Sinaloa, these nine families of Spanish, Mexican-Indian and Negro descent, destined in history as the founding settlers of El Pueblo de la Reina de Los Angeles, the City of the Angels.

They had been recruited by Captain Fernando Rivera y Moncada specifically for the establishment of a pueblo on fertile land near the Rio de Porciuncula (now the Los Angeles River).

These Pobladores, as they were called, traveled by sea from Los Alamos on the mainland to Loreto on the Baja peninsula. From there, they continued by muletrain to Mission Santa Maria on the Baja coast. Then, they followed the coast to San Diego, San Juan Capistrano, San Gabriel and finally the site of the new pueblo.

Along with the colonists settled at Pueblo de San Jose de Guadalupe, they were expected by their government to become farmers, selling their crops to the California presidios at San Diego, Santa Barbara, Monterey and San Francisco. In addition to pueblo lots, they were provided nearby farmland.

By 1831, the year Romualdo Pacheco was born, Bancroft estimated that 770 persons lived in Los Angeles. Another 230 people occupied nearby ranchos. The Indian population in the area had fallen from several thousand to 150-350. Another 150-175 people lived around Missions San Gabriel and San Fernando. Sources other than Bancroft claim somewhat larger numbers in all these categories.

While Pacheco was lieutenant governor, a vigilante group captured Tiburcio Vasquez near Los Angeles and took him to San Jose for hanging.

At the time Pacheco became governor in 1875, the Southern Pacific tracks through the inland valley between the bay area in the north and Los Angeles were still incomplete. However, the first train reached Los Angeles in 1876. By this time, the city had an estimated population of about 6000 people. Local business people felt guardedly optimistic about the future growth and prosperity of there dusty little city.

THE MEXICAN-AMERICAN WHO WON

FOUNDING FAMILIES OF LOS ANGELES LEAVING DESCENDANTS

1. Jose Fernando de Velasco y Lara with wife Maria Regina Antonia Campos and children Josef Julian, Maria Juana de Jesus, and Maria Faustina.

2. Josef Moreno with wife Maria Gertrudis Perez.

3. Jose Antonio Navarro with wife Maria Regina Dorotea Gloria de Soto y Rodriguez and children Josef Maria Eduardo, Josef Clemente, Mariana Josefa.

4. Luis Quintero with wife Maria Petra Rubio and children Maria Concepcion, Maria Tomasa, Maria Rafaela, Josef Clemente, and Maria Gertrudis Castelo, adopted.

5. Pablo Rodriguez with wife Maria Rosalia Noriega and daughter Maria Antonia.

6. Jose Vanegas with wife Maria Bonifacia Maxima Aguilar and son Cosme Damien.

7. Jose Antonio Basilio Rosas with wife Maria Manuela Calistra Hernandez and children Alejandro, Josef Maximo, Josef Carlos, Antonio Rosalino, Josef Marcelino, Juan Esteban, Maria Josefa.

8. Jose Alejandro Rosas with wife Juana Maria Rodriguez.

9. Antonio Clemente Feliz Villavicencio with wife Maria de los Santos Serefina Flores and adopted daughter, Maria Antonia Josefa Pinuelas.

The escolta or guard of the new pueblo included Corporal Vicente Feliz, Antonio Cota, Roque Cota and Francisco Lugo.

*

ROMUALDO PACHECO'S CALIFORNIA

from page 65

role as a politician provided ready entrance into elite social circles. California writers of Mrs. Pacheco's time as well as in future years lauded her achievements. Just as her husband pioneered new paths for hispanics, she took historic first steps on behalf of California women.

The Daily Alta California carried this brief notice about their wedding: "Hon. Romualdo Pacheco, State Treasurer, has found a treasure at the very threshold of his official career."

They soon started a family. First came their daughter, Maybella Ramona, and then a son, also Romualdo. Unfortunately, the boy died in early childhood. In future years, Maybella married William Tevis, the son of a San Francisco banker, Lloyd Tevis.(45)

Although the record provides no date, Pacheco eventually joined his wife as a member of the Episcopal Church. Soon after, he became a Mason.(46) These decisions appear as a culmination of various lifelong influences: his childhood years in a protestant school, his anglo-protestant wife's religious preference, and perhaps even some notion that his own political career might be enhanced by the change.

Pacheco Faces A New Political Foe

If Pacheco really thought his career in public life might be advanced by a change in church, he faced a deeply disturbing irony.

In 1867, with the war ended, he was again a candidate for state treasurer. But now, for the first time in his career, he found himself competing for office against another Californio, Antonio F. Coronel of Los Angeles, a man faithful to the catholic church and running on the

STOCKTON, MID-19TH CENTURY- This San Joaquin river town, because of its connection to San Francisco Bay, became an important settlement in early California. A fire destroyed its irregular design in 1850. Soon after, it was properly laid out and named to honor Commodore Robert Stockton who in 1846 served as the territory's second military governor.

THE MEXICAN-AMERICAN WHO WON

democratic ticket.

Coronel had accumulated some wealth along with social and political power in Southern California. Now, 50 years old, he sought his first statewide political office. He and his father, Ignacio, had arrived in California from Mexico in 1834 with the Hijar and Padres Colony. At the time, Antonio was 17 years old.

His father was a teacher who eventually set up a school in Los Angeles. Given his family background, it's likely that Coronel's education was far superior to most Californians of the day, including most Americans.

During his young manhood, he served in the Mexican military in California and held various administrative positions in Los Angeles. In 1846, Governor Pio Pico granted him Rancho Sierra de los Verdugos. When the United States military first occupied and temporarily lost Los Angeles to the Californios, Coronel fought against the Americans as a captain in the Mexican military.(48)

Pacheco had attached himself to the Republican-Union coalition during the last election, so his affiliation and commitment continued in this new campaign for office.

The Democrats nominated Henry Haight for governor, a man of good political reputation. In the political climate following the Civil War, it scarcely seemed a race for the Democrats. Neither the Union nor the Republican Parties had

SACRAMENTO CITY, 1854- The steamboat landing as it appeared when viewed from the Sacramento River. Romualdo Pacheco arrived at this landing to serve his first term as state senator in 1858.

ROMUALDO PACHECO'S CALIFORNIA

CIRCA 1851, FRONT STREET, SACRAMENTO- Heavy flooding nearly every year soon required that buildings close to the Sacramento and American Rivers be raised.

strength enough alone to win or even make a good showing, and they did not work well together after the war. Both went down in defeat.

Coronel defeated Romualdo Pacheco by less than 3000 votes statewide, and for the first time in years, Pacheco was without a political position.(49)

Pacheco's burdens were made worse with the death of his brother, Mariano, and his eldest half-sister, Ignacio. It was a time of grief for him, his mother and the other children. He had pushed himself very hard for a number of years, and now everything seemed lost.

If he hoped to return to state politics, he had no choice but to start over again, making a run for the state senate in the 1869 election. By now, he was a driven man. He had no choice.

It would be the toughest election he had ever faced. The incumbent was Patrick Murphy, a very aggressive fighter. He owned the great 17,735-acre Santa Margarita rancho as well as a portion of the Asuncion and other rancho lands in the northern part of San Luis Obispo County. (50)

Murphy immediately challenged Pacheco's integrity in an open letter first published in the San Luis Obispo Pioneer and then reprinted in the San Luis Obispo Tribune, saying, "Being anxious..to expose and hold up to public condemnation those gross political heresies of which you are understood to be champion..I..invite you to accompany me through the district, and to discuss with me,

THE MEXICAN-AMERICAN WHO WON

both in English and Spanish, the issues involved."

Romualdo's longstanding reputation as a gentlemanly person along with his deftness as a politician led him to write his own public letter declining Murphy's invitation to debate. "I would scarcely feel at liberty to accept it, since your avowed purpose is..to expose and hold (me) up to public condemnation..." Pacheco wrote.

"It is my wish," he continued, "that you..do what you consider your duty, unembarrassed by my presence which would, I fear, act as a check upon the eloquence of a gentleman of your well-known modesty and delicate consideration for the feelings of others."

People who knew Murphy surely saw Pacheco's remarks as a real put-down because Murphy was not known either for his delicacy or modesty. The Tribune published these letters in both English and Spanish.

In this same issue, the editor described his feeling about Pacheco. First, he told about Pacheco's past experience. Then, he added, that Pacheco could be counted upon for "his uniformly urbane and gentlemanly demeanor, the strictness and impartiality with which he fulfilled his duties..and his well-known independence of..influences and intrigues..(He) has such a host of friends to speak for him that he needs no eulogy at our hands.

"We will..say, from a long and intimate acquaintance with him, that we know him to be a man of the most polished manners, of a kind and courteous disposition, of upright conduct, of unblemished honor, of liberal education and of much more than ordinary intellect.

"With all (his) affection for his native compatriots (he has) the still greater merit, that his perfect assimilation with the (Americans) enables him to occupy the position of peacemaker between the two-often discordant races..Such men are scarce on both sides, Spanish or American, and when found, should

PONY EXPRESS RIDER ARRIVES IN SACRAMENTO- This mail service between St. Joseph, Missouri and Sacramento, California operated for only 18 months. The 1800 mile journey required 10 days.

be cherished by both sides."(51)

Undoubtedly, this writer's description of Pacheco won votes for him, but if the September 1, 1869 election results in San Luis Obispo County had determined the election, Pacheco would have lost by 68 votes. Fortunately, the community of his birth, Santa Barbara, favored him by a larger margin. He won the election by eight votes.

Murphy immediately challenged the count, charging fraud, inaccuracies and undue influence at the polls. This challenge continued throughout the next session of the Senate. It actually came to ballot in the legislature several times, each official voting with his party. The vote was always a tie. Pacheco's election was finally confirmed by a legislative vote of 20-19. (52)

However close, this election brought Pacheco back to Sacramento and the center of the state's political action, and he enjoyed a great deal of recognition among members of his party and members of the legislature.

Talk of Romualdo Pacheco As Governor

In 1871, Michel de Young, publisher of the San Francisco Chronicle and a solid Republican, reviewed his earlier predictions about who were likely candidates for governor. Among those named, he included General John F. Miller, Romualdo Pacheco, Newton Booth, Eugene Sullivan and R. W. Roberts.

One by one, the Chronicle reviewed the background of these men, and finally decided Newton Booth was the most likely winner.

Page 86 please

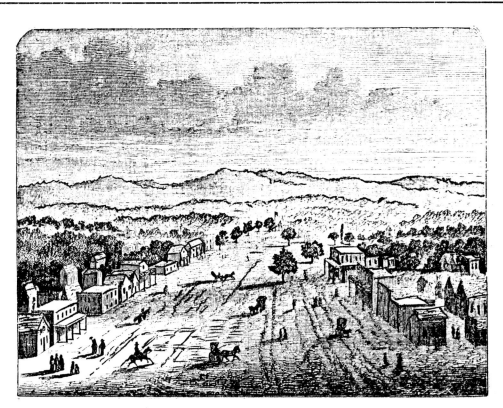

SACRAMENTO STREET SCENE, 1850'S

THE MEXICAN-AMERICAN WHO WON

ROUNDING CAPE HORN

Sailors aboard early ships rounding the tip of South America into the Pacific Ocean recalled this scene near Point Arenas, a place for taking on stores. They experienced days of cold Antarctica weather, rough seas and seasickness. Heavy clouds, rain, fiords and ice greeted them through the Strait of Magellan. (Harper's New Monthly Magazine, Volume 1871-72)

1863 C. P. R. R. 1869

GRAND
RAILROAD CELEBRATION

IN HONOR OF THE COMPLETION OF THE

GREAT NATIONAL RAILWAY

ACROSS THE CONTINENT.

The Completion of this Great Work will be Celebrated in Sacramento, on the

EIGHTH DAY OF MAY, 1869,

Under the Direction of the COMMITTEE of CITIZENS

Chosen for that Purpose.

H. S. Crocker & Co's Print, Sac.

THE MEXICAN-AMERICAN WHO WON

SIDEBAR STORY 8

INTERIOR OF SNOW-SHED.

CENTRAL PACIFIC TRAIN IN SNOW SHED

"Promontory Summit, May 10, 1869, 12 Midnight- To the press East and West: The last rail is laid...the last spike driven! The Pacific Railroad is completed to the point of junction, 1086 miles west of the Missouri River and 690 miles from Sacramento."

This triumphant telegram reached Sacramento, San Francisco and San Jose almost simultaneously. It came from Leland Stanford, president of the Central Pacific Railroad, and T.C.Durant, an official of the Union Pacific Railroad. It was at Promontory Point that they had met and joined the track of these two companies.

ROMUALDO PACHECO'S CALIFORNIA

Since 1859 when a Pacific Railroad Convention was held in San Francisco, the hope for a transcontinental rail line was part of an effervescent nineteenth century California dream. Now, at last, it had happened. But it had been a long suffering struggle. The completion of this track was the great technological wonder of nineteenth century America.

One great hero in the railroad drama was an engineer named Theodore Judah. Some people saw him as a fanatic, but he believed deeply in the reality of this line.

Way back when Romualdo Pacheco assumed the duties of County Judge in San Luis Obispo County, Judah made it to California by ship to work as chief engineer for C. L. Wilson, a man who wanted a railroad built from Sacramento to a placer mining district in the Sierra foothills. Judah oversaw construction of this 27-mile Sacramento Valley Railroad into Placer County, the first line in California.

Even while this work took place, Judah talked about building a railroad "from sea to shining sea." He became bewitched by his dream. In 1859, he played a leading role at the San Francisco Convention in explaining how this railroad could be built. On the strength of his conviction and the knowledge he possessed, the convention sent him to Washington D.C. to seek federal support. Congressman John Burch from California said of Judah, "His knowledge of his subject was so thorough, his manners so gentle...his conversation...so entertaining that few could resist his appeals." But the Congress had too many other problems. They did not place the railroad upon the agenda that year.

Back in California, Judah went into the Sierras with helpers to establish, as far as possible, a definite railroad route. In Sacramento, he called a meeting for all who might be interested. He distributed his pamphlets, showed his maps and painted a picture of unbelievable profits. Four Sacramento merchants sat in the audience...Leland Stanford, a grocer; Charles Crocker, a dry goods store owner; Collis Huntington and Mark Hopkins, partners in a hardware store. They agreed to back Judah in building 18 miles of line and to financially support his return to Washington, D.C. to continue the campaign for government financial support.

All of these men had found their way to California and into business in Sacramento during the gold rush. They were tentatively committing themselves to the greatest construction feat this country had ever known.

With the Civil War, railroads suddenly assumed new importance. Congress and Abraham Lincoln signed a bill July 1, 1862 designating the

THE MEXICAN-AMERICAN WHO WON

SNOW-SHEDS ON THE PACIFIC RAILROAD.

new Central Pacific Railroad, under control of these Sacramento merchants, and the Union Pacific in Missouri as builders of the transcontinental line.

Leland Stanford, president of Central Pacific, was also governor of California. He was in a position to obtain many concessions for his company. But soon, disagreements developed between Judah and his backers. Judah, the man who had conceived the dream and worked so hard to make it reality was forced out of the company in its earliest stages. While crossing the Isthmus of Panama enroute to the East to seek support from others, he caught yellow fever. He died in New York November 2, 1863, but railroad construction continued along the route he had laid out.

Stanford was a very public man who enjoyed the influence of public office. In later years, his only son died. He and Mrs. Stanford devoted much of the rest of their lives to the establishment of Leland Stanford, Jr. University at Palo Alto, California.

Colis P. Huntington dominated the operation of Central Pacific, first as vice president and later as president of the company. His biographers describe him as extremely hard, anti-social, cold, crafty and frequently dishonest.

Charles Crocker was in charge of actual construction. The thousands of Chinese workers along the railroad bed called him "Chollie Clocker." The railroad received $18,000 per mile for track on flatland, and as much as $48,000 per mile in the mountains. They paid their Chinese labor $40 per month.

With the technology that came in later years, it is now hard to believe that this entire railroad line through the Sierra-Nevada mountains was built without power tools, scrapers or dynamite. Picks, shovels, one-horse dump carts, wheelbarrels and black powder were their tools for building railroad beds. A portion of the line was constructed through solid rock at the rate of one-inch per day.

Five hundred persons were present at Promontory Point in Utah to celebrate completion of the line. Stanford served a luncheon aboard his private car to a small group of dignitaries. That evening everyone enjoyed a banquet, a grand ball and a torchlight procession. Stanford's telegram to the press in California set off a jubilant celebration that reverberated the length of the state. The westward movement by covered wagon had been replaced by a much more comfortable mode of transcontinental transporation.

THE MEXICAN-AMERICAN WHO WON

George Pullman

George M. Pullman was inventor and holder of patents for the ingenious devices that made up his luxurious bedroom and dining cars. By 1872, he owned 500 sleeping, drawing room and dining cars serving railroads on 100 routes. During those years, American trains became the ultimate in comfort and service, surpassing most trains in Europe. (Harper's New Monthly Magazine, May 1872)

ROMUALDO PACHECO'S CALIFORNIA

DINING-ROOM, UNION PACIFIC RAILROAD.

THE PULLMAN HOTEL CAR of the 1870's seated 40 persons at its tables. It was a time of Victorian splendor with plush upholstered seats, curtained windows, carpeted floors and silver plate service. (Harper's New Monthly Magazine, May, 1872)

THE MEXICAN-AMERICAN WHO WON

INTERIOR OF PULLMAN SLEEPING CAR, PACIFIC RAILROAD.

UPHOLSTERED SEATS OPENED into berths for sleeping. Porters made up the beds with crisp white sheets and pillows with feather ticking. Here, an 1870's mother tucks her child in bed while a dowager in dark cape and headcovering dozes sitting upright. (Harper's New Monthly Magazine, May, 1872)

ROMUALDO PACHECO'S CALIFORNIA

INTERIOR OF A PULLMAN PALACE CAR, PACIFIC RAILROAD.

PULLMAN REFERRED TO HIS LUXURIOUSLY ornamented cars as Palace Cars. Travelers in this scene are shown dressed for elegant travel...men in top hats, women and children wearing coats and hats. A solicitous conductor seeks assurance that his women travelers are comfortable. (Harper's New Monthly Magazine, May, 1872)

THE MEXICAN-AMERICAN WHO WON

DINING-ROOM, UNION PACIFIC RAILROAD.

These early cars also included a wine closet, a linen closet and lockers with sufficient provisions to feed forty people "all the way from Chicago to the Pacific."
(Harper's New Monthly Magazine, May, 1872)

PULLMAN KITCHENS WERE A marvel of compactness with sink, hot and cold running water faucets and "every modern convenience."

COOKING RANGE, PULLMAN PALACE CAR, UNION PACIFIC RAILROAD.

ROMUALDO PACHECO'S CALIFORNIA

1850'S- A CHINESE MINER, a merchant and coolie and a Chinese gambling den.

THE MEXICAN-AMERICAN WHO WON

CHINESE IN CALIFORNIA SIDEBAR STORY 9

Chinese migrants arriving in California from 1848 to 1852 faced the worst possible racial tolerance. From the time gold was first discovered in the territory, they arrived, so unique and foreign in appearance and language that neither Anglos nor Californios accepted them. At a date some years in the future even Romualdo Pacheco appeared before Congress on behalf of a bill to exclude further Chinese from entering the country.

The Chinese patiently submitted to cuffing, name calling and allowing themselves to be used like slaves in the gold mines. Years later, they served as the principal laborers in the construction of the Central Pacific Railroad. Anglos referred to them as "John Chinaman" and "coolies".

But the migration continued. By 1852, the Annals of San Francisco estimated the Chinese population in California at between 16,000 and 20,000. In San Francisco, some 3000-4000 quartered themselves along upper Sacramento Street and the full length of Dupont Street. A group of Chinese merchants became wealthy catering to their own alienated citizens.

Thousands of Chinese scattered into towns and settlements all of the way south to San Diego. Nearly every community of size had its Chinatown.

ROMUALDO PACHECO'S CALIFORNIA

from page 72

Booth's stand against government subsidy and monopoly practices of the railroads was most persuasive, and he projected an extraordinary sense of integrity and fairness in all matters.(53)

The evening before the Republican Convention took place at Mercantile Library Hall in San Francisco, Booth arrived from Sacramento aboard the Steamer Chrysolis. The Young Republicans were waiting for him. They escorted him from the steamer to a waiting carriage drawn by six white horses. Professor Gilliard, a black man,

JULY 16, 1871- ROMUALDO PACHECO WAS A CANDIDATE FOR LIEUTENANT GOVERNOR OF CALIFORNIA as running mate with Newton Booth who sought the governorship. As members of the Republican Party, they ran in opposition to Governor Henry Haight. Here, the San Francisco Chronicle shows Booth decrying Haight's lavish expenditures from the state contingency fund.

THE MEXICAN-AMERICAN WHO WON

carried blue-flamed gaslights alongside the carriage. People jammed the streets, the Chronicle reported, as Booth waved to the crowd, and Young Republican's led the line of march along Davis, Washington and Montgomery Streets. Fireworks lighted the way. A speaking platform had been erected in front of the Grand Hotel on New Montgomery Street, and a band played as Booth took his place at the lectern. It was an exhilarating moment.(54) Romualdo Pacheco was also in town and had reason to enjoy the excitement.

All other prospects for the Republican nomination for governor, diminished in the clamor for Booth. At the time, he was a 45-year-old bachelor. He had once practiced law, but was drawn to California and Sacramento during the gold rush where he established a highly successful mercantile store. He had served only one term as a state senator, but he had a statesman-like demeanor that could not be denied. He was slender, only 5-feet, 8-inches tall. Through his sandy brown beard, his easy smile pleased people. (55)

Romualdo Pacheco Recognized

At the convention the next day Booth easily won the nomination on

A Prophetic View of the Mill that is to take place September 6th.

IN THIS FRONT PAGE POLITICAL CARTOON, the San Francisco Chronicle predicts that Governor Henry Haight will take a real beating from Newton Booth. As Booth's running mate, Romualdo Pacheco used his strength to gain votes with the Spanish speaking people.

ROMUALDO PACHECO'S CALIFORNIA

THIS POLITICAL CARTOON depicts Governor Henry Haight as a devilish heathen peering down from the stack of ledgers representing California's indebtedness during his administration. He is surrounded by cronies of the confederacy.

the first ballot, and as Pacheco hoped, he found himself a nominee for lieutenant governor in competition with Senator E. W. Roberts. As it became clear to Roberts that Pacheco had the largest following, he withdrew from nomination. Pacheco also won the nomination on the first ballot.

The Democratic Party nominated the incumbent Henry Haight as their candidate for governor with E. J. Lewis as nominee for lieutenant governor. The Chronicle described Pacheco's opponent as "an ornate and lofty man." (56)

It became Romualdo Pacheco's

THE MEXICAN-AMERICAN WHO WON

role during the campaign to attract the vote of the Californios and convince the people of his district and surrounding districts to vote the Republican ticket.

Neither Pacheco nor his opponent received attention from the press. As the Chronicle said in support of its candidate for governor, "The Republicans bet all the money they had..on Booth's carrying San Francisco and the state." (57)

Republicans Elected

And so it happened. California elected a Californio for lieutenant governor. Romualdo Pacheco had been the right man at the right place at the right time. For years, he had walked a narrow line, seldom expressing views so firmly as to create opposition; seldom arousing potential political enemies. His cousin, Pablo de la Guerra, had succeeded to lieutenant governor

Page 91 please

AS CAMPAIGN NEARED THE END, this cartoon showed Newton Booth easily rowing toward the new capitol building while the Governor falls behind. The governor carries the stigma of having signed a lottery bill, paying off a street commissioner, subsidizing railroads.

ROMUALDO PACHECO'S CALIFORNIA

JULY 23, 1871- A LONG LINE of Irish and German immigrants wait to vote for Newton Booth while Governor Henry Haight cohorts with confederates, hooligans and the town character known as Emperor Norton. (San Francisco Chronicle)

THE MEXICAN-AMERICAN WHO WON

SAN FRANCISCO, CAL., SUNDAY, AUGUST 27, 1871

September Sixth the sun is low—
Poor Haight has many lengths to go;

But Booth is in across the score—
And Haight can never venture more.

from page 89

from state senate speaker when the position had opened midterm, but Pacheco was the first Californio to stand for statewide election for such high office.

Pacheco As Senate President

As lieutenant governor, Pacheco also served as president of the senate. He took his seat as president of this body on Monday, September 10, 1871. Under ordinary circumstances, he might have played an important role in making appointments to senate committees, and in this way, exercised more power in the legislature. However, three days before he came to duty, the holdover Democrats from the 1869 election called a session. By two votes, they still enjoyed a majority vote in the chamber. At this early session, they adopted a rule calling for "all senate committees and joint house committees" to be appointed by the Senate membership. One can wonder whether this act hurt the new lieutenant governor's pride or

Page 93 please

SAN FRANCISCO CHRONICLE, TUESDAY, JULY

THE CHAMPIONS OF WOMAN SUFFRAGE.

SUSAN B. ANTHONY.

ELIZABETH CADY STANTON.

THE FEMALE AGITATORS

The Great Woman Suffrage Champions Here.

Interview with a Chronicle Reporter.

BIOGRAPHICAL SKETCHES OF MRS. STANTON AND MISS ANTHONY.

POLITICAL CARTOON—Two champions of women's suffrage arrived in San Francisco in July, 1871, while the state election campaign was underway. They stayed at the Grand Hotel, received the press in their suite and talked to a number of women's groups about women's rights. (San Francisco Chronicle, July, 1871)

THE MEXICAN-AMERICAN WHO WON

from page 91

whether he simply viewed it as an inevitable political act. Whatever he thought, he did not react.

In the course of events, he recognized his helplessness as a Republican in a chamber where the Democrats were in the majority. Without explanation, he took leave, turning his duties to the Senate President Pro Tem William Irwin, a Democrat, for the last 60 days of the first session.

But as exofficio warden of the state prison and chairman of a committee to select a site for a new prison, he played an active role in determining where Folsom Prison, not named at the time, would be located. The site selected was near a rock quarry, and prisoners from San Quentin were used to quarry the rock for the new buildings and outside walls.(58)

At the beginning of the legislative term in 1873, Pacheco again assumed his duties as presiding officer in the Senate, carrying an important message from the governor that might bear upon his own future.

Just before the first meeting of the legislators in 1873, Gov. Newton Booth received a telegraphed letter dated November 28 from U.S. Senator Eugene Casserly announcing his immediate resignation. It read, in part: "My public duties on both sides of the continent have demanded of me and have received so much attention as to greatly impair my health..I have deferred carrying out my desire (to resign) until..the Legislature, just about to meet, may elect my successor." (59)

Casserly was a good Democrat. By waiting until this time to announce his resignation, the legislature could choose his

Page 98 please

SUNDAY, SEPTEMBER 3, 1871.

REPUBLICAN STATE TICKET.

For Governor,
NEWTON BOOTH.

For Lieutenant-Governor,
ROMUALDO PACHECO.

For Secretary of State,
DRURY MELONE.

For Judge of the Supreme Court—
(LONG TERM).
A. L. RHODES.

For Judge of the Supreme Court—
(SHORT TERM.)
A. C. NILES.

For Controller,
JAMES J. GREEN.

For Treasurer,
FERDINAND BAEHR.

For Surveyor-General,
ROBERT GARDNER.

For Attorney-General,
JOHN L. LOVE.

For Clerk of the Supreme Court,
GRANT I. TAGGART.

For State Printer,
THOMAS A. SPRINGER.

For Harbor Commissioner,
JOHN A. McGLYNN.

For Superintendent of Public Instruction,
HENRY M. BOLANDER.

CONGRESSIONAL TICKET.

FOR CONGRESS.
First District,
S. O. HOUGHTON.

Second District,
A. A. SARGENT.

Third District,
JOHN M. COGHLAN.

LEGISLATIVE TICKET.

For Joint Senator,
SELDON J. FINNEY.

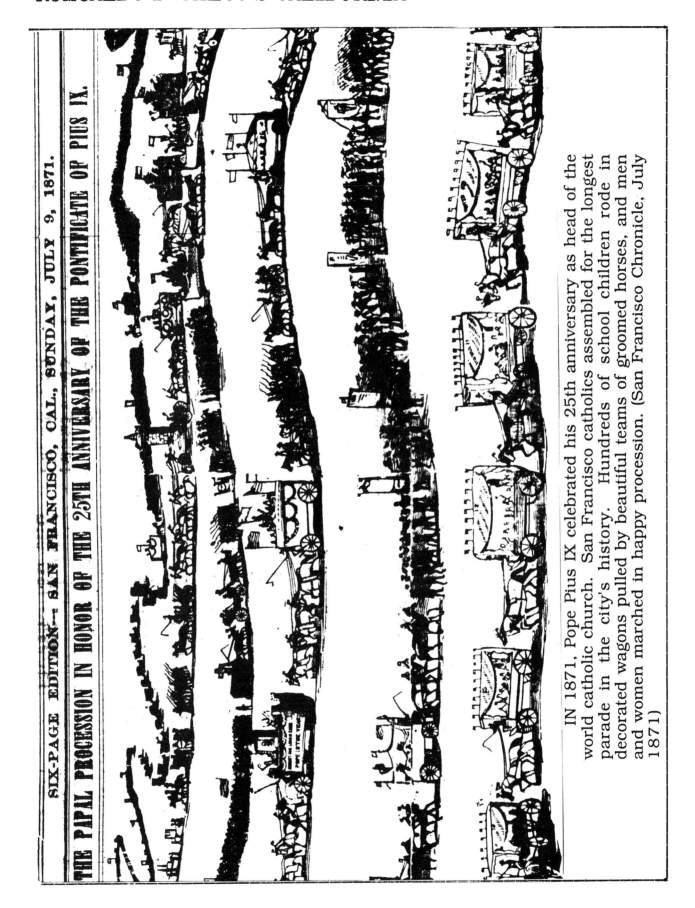

IN 1871, Pope Pius IX celebrated his 25th anniversary as head of the world catholic church. San Francisco catholics assembled for the longest parade in the city's history. Hundreds of school children rode in decorated wagons pulled by beautiful teams of groomed horses, and men and women marched in happy procession. (San Francisco Chronicle, July 1871)

THE INAUGURAL BALL.

Feminine Perplexities and Masculine Dilemmas.

DAZZLING SCENE AT THE CAPITOL

TERPSICHORE IN THE HALLS OF THE SOLONS.

WHO WAS THE BELLE OF THE BALL?

[SPECIAL DISPATCH TO THE CHRONICLE.]

SACRAMENTO, December 19, 1871.

An Inaugural ball occurs in California once every four years. It can't very well happen more frequently, because a Gubernatorial Inauguration transpires only once every four years according to law and the Constitution. Whenever the Legislature meets a grand ball is given, but such entertainments are not supposed to equal in magnificence and splendor a regular Inauguration affair. The present ball, given in honor of the installation of Governor Newton Booth and the Republican Administration, has occupied the attention of the citizens of Sacramento for several weeks past, for upon them specially is it incumbent to see that all Inaugural balls are successes. With the ladies through the entire State the question, "To go or not to go?" has been paramount.

LEGISLATIVE PROCEEDINGS.

Senate.

SACRAMENTO, December 11, 1871.

Lieutenant-Governor Pacheco was present for the first time in the Senate, which was called to order at 2 o'clock. Mr. Pacheco made the following remarks:

"I fully realize the solemnity of the oath which, in accordance with law, was administered and taken by me on the 8th instant. It shall be my highest ambition to justify the generous trust reposed in me by those whose suffrages have placed me here, and to merit and possess the confidence of this entire body by an impartial discharge of the duties devolving upon me as your presiding officer. I feel sure it will be unnecessary for me to appeal to the members of this Senate for the courtesy and patience that will make my duties less difficult; that they will generously yield it to one who will strive in every way to deserve their approval, I am fully confident. In conclusion permit me to express the hope that the session upon which we are now entering will be characterized by wise and moderate legislation. Let the interests of those who sent us here and the welfare of the State at large ever be sacredly considered; and, moreover, let each member of this body resolve that he will do his utmost toward making the nineteenth session of the Legislature of California the most profitable our State has yet known."

Senator Evans was then called upon to preside, Mr. Pacheco's absence being necessary.

Mr. Irwin introduced an amendment to the Constitution to tax all property except public schools, etc.

Mr. Larkin introduced a resolution providing for public schools eight months in the year.

A Committee resolution that the Judiciary Committee of both Houses act as a Joint Committee in the revision of the Code was adopted.

Mr. Maclay offered a resolution granting the use of the Senate Chamber for the Inaugural Ball, which was adopted.

The Senate then adjourned.

SENATOR BOOTH.

The People Triumphant.

The Victory Won on the First Ballot Yesterday.

Booth, 61; Farley, [...]; ter, 20; Irwin[...]

Klotz, McCune a[nd ...] Vote for Bo[oth]

Senator Booth Keeps Open House and Receives the Congratulations of Men of all Parties.

Finis Coronat Opus—the end crowns the work. The election of Governor Newton Booth to be United States Senator is a fitting end to the work done by the people since September last, and is a lesson taught the professional politicians and time servers which will not soon be forgotten.

THE QUIET INFLUENCE OF PACHECO is discernible in the convention of Graves and the probable enlistment of Escandon. Pacheco wants to be Governor, if only for the fag end of Booth's term.

ROMUALDO PACHECO'S CALIFORNIA

from page 93

replacement. If he had resigned before the meeting of the legislature, Gov. Booth would have undoubtedly appointed someone of his choice and party to fill the unexpired term. But Gov. Booth had his agenda too.

*****

Governor Booth Makes Bid for U.S. Senate

During these years, United States Senators were elected by both houses of the state legislature rather than by popular vote. The 1873 session of the legislature must now elect one senator to fill Casserly's term through February, 1875, and elect another for a six-year term beginning in 1875. Or the same man could be elected for both terms, but the legislators showed no inclination toward this possibility. All three parties active at the time pushed candidates for both positions, but none alone had the strength to elect. There had to be some kind of coalition.

Sometime earlier, Gov. Booth had let many legislators know that he would seek election to the six-year term as U.S. Senator which would begin immediately upon completion of his term as governor, so his hat was already in the ring. The Democrats, the railroad people and certainly Casserly bitterly opposed Booth.

If Lt. Gov. Romualdo Pacheco felt some special excitement about Booth's possible election to the U. S. Senate, it was easy to understand. Booth's election should mean his resignation as governor. Maybe, just maybe, a Californio could make it to the highest office in the state by automatic succession. Pacheco would certainly use all of the political strength he could muster to help Booth.

Governor Booth Becomes United States Senator.

Governor Booth has resigned his position as chief magistrate of California, and he will fill his position in the Senate of the United States upon its opening on the 5th of next month. ROMUALDO PACHECO has been sworn in as acting Governor until his successor, who must in the meantime be elected, shall be entitled to receive the office, upon the first Monday of next December. The Lieutenant-Governor will bring to the position a large experience gained by a long and intimate knowledge of our State affairs. His high personal and political character is a guarantee of the faithful and intelligent performance of the duties of his office. Mr. Irwin of Siskiyou, as President of the Senate, becomes Lieutenant-Governor and ex officio Warden of the State Prison.

FEBRUARY 28, 1875,

S.F. Chronicle

THE MEXICAN-AMERICAN WHO WON

Gov. Booth provided most newspapers with an advance telegraphed resume of his planned annual message before the joint legislature. He told California voters that he remained firm in opposing subsidies to the railroads and all other monopoly corporations that might seek such help from the government. He felt that railroad passenger and freight rates must be controlled by law and that companies should be compelled to post their rates in every station. He favored elimination of capital punishment and regarded printing of state laws in Spanish as an unneccessary expense. His platform, not at all new, remained immensely popular with his supporters. (60)

December 1, 1873 in Sacramento found legislators and lobbyists in conference at nearly all principal hotels. Booth's supporters opened rooms on Front Street for all who sought information about his program and plans if elected to the U.S. Senate. Billy Carr, a lawyer and lobbyist for the Atlantic and Pacific Railroad Company, took public rooms in the Orleans Hotel near the Capitol and provided free meals to all legislators who visited. Casserly, the resigned senator, took up quarters in the Democrat's rooms to fight against the election of Booth.(61)

On December 12, the Chronicle again carried a strong editorial in support of Booth. "Both Governor Booth and the Chronicle saw the gigantic evils of monopolies threatening the public weal," the newspaper reminded its readers.(62)

******

Lieutenant Governor Pacheco Guides Election Process

Late in December the legislators still had not elected U.S. Senators for either the short term or long term, but all of them wanted to conclude the battle before the holiday recess. To speed the process, Lt. Gov. Pacheco called for a midday joint session of the Senate and the Assembly to take a vote for candidates nominated for the six-year term. This count showed 57 votes for Booth, 41 for Farley and 21 votes for Shafter. Booth needed only three more votes for a majority, but the hardened allegiance of legislators to their parties made any change extremely difficult.

Before the next joint session, Pacheco talked to several legislators. The Chronicle reported, "The quiet influence of Pacheco is discernable in the conversation with Graves and the probable enlistment of Escandon. Pacheco wants to be governor, if only for the fag end of Booth's term." (63)

On December 20, Pacheco, probably feeling he had done all of the behind the scenes work that he could do, called for another joint session of the Senate and Assembly. Graves was the Democratic senator from Pacheco's home district. Apart from politics, they had known each other for years. But Graves had made a commitment that was difficult to break. In an earlier party caucus, he had initiated a pledge morally binding all Democrats to vote as a block. As the meeting of the legislature came to order, there was no way to know whether he had received a release from his party's stand.

"The gallery was filled with spectators and several ladies

occupied seats," the Chronicle reported. Many legislators took this occasion to express their views, and "the proceedings were often interrupted by cheers and well-meant applause."

Using his gavel, Pacheco found it necessary to call for order several times. The balloting must have seemed interminably long that day. As the roll was called, each legislator stood to discuss the rationale for his vote. When Grave's turn came, everyone was waiting. To the surprise of many, he did not make a speech. He simply stood, looked directly at Pacheco, and called out, "I cast my vote for Newton Booth."

With that, the cheering started. Pacheco allowed it to run its course. Before the balloting ended, Escandon of Ventura and McCune of Solano also changed their votes to Booth. This brought the vote for Booth to 60. One more vote would give him a clear lead.

When Klotz, a Democrat from Shasta, was called upon to vote, he stood. "The silence of death prevailed in the chamber," the Chronicle said. They quoted Klotz as saying, "I originally favored re-electing Casserly. Since there is no chance..I cast my vote for Booth."

When the balloting was completed, only a confirming announcement of the tally was needed. The secretary gave Pacheco the count, and he read: "Whole number of votes cast, 119; necessary to a choice, 60. Of these, Farley received 37; Shafter, 20; Irwin, 1; and Booth...61!"

Above the cheers and shouting, Pacheco call out, "With Newton Booth, having received a majority of all votes cast, I hearby declare him duly elected Senator of the United States for the term of six years commencing March 4, 1875."

All of the cheering, excitement and congratulations were for Governor Booth, but as Pacheco quietly laid down the gavel and took a deep breath, he must have felt a surge of excitement for himself. That evening he joined others in Booth's rooms on Front Street to add his congratulations.

As the Chronicle reported, "Lt. Gov. Pacheco must be right glad that he is to be Governor for a while."

Among Republicans, his name was already being mentioned as a candidate for govenor in 1875. But could that be? Was it possible that the party would risk its chance of gaining the governorship by nominating a Californio? The racial intolerance of those years made it seem improbable. (64)

Democrat John S. Hager, readily known for his support of the railroads, became the strongest contender for the short term position as U.S. Senator. Billy Carr threw all of his support and plenty of money into the election of Hagar, and the Democrats went along with him because they desperately wanted to get something out of this protracted legislative flap. Hagar was elected.

*****
A Disappointing Wait..

The next year or so after that session must have seemed very ambiguous and uncomfortable for Romualdo Pacheco. After Newton Booth's election as U.S. Senator, most people assumed that he would immediately resign the governorship, but he didn't. In fact, it became clear that he intended to remain in that office for as long as possible. Officially, his term as U.S. Senator would not begin until March 4, 1875. For an ambitious and

THE MEXICAN-AMERICAN WHO WON

hopeful Pacheco, this situation was heartrending. He could be kept completely out of the governor's chair. But whatever he felt, he remained silent, publicly championing Booth all of the way.

However, Senator Philip A. Roach, San Francisco, led a group who felt that Booth should resign. He even proposed an amendment to the state constitution to make California governors ineligible for any other elective office during their term. It was not adopted at the time, but it later became law under Section 20 of Article V of the new constitution at the 1878-79 convention. After all, Booth's critics said, when Governor Milton Latham was elected U.S. Senator in 1860, he resigned. It became apparent to some elected officials that Booth might even consider delaying going to Washington for the first session of Congress in order to hold the governorship until the end of his term. (65)

But, at long last, fate worked in Pacheco's favor. Something occurred that neither he nor his friends anticipated. It opened the way for Romualdo Pacheco's unique place in California history.

The Chronicle reported it this way: "When Governor Booth was first elected, it was under the pledge to perform the duties of the Gubernatorial office to the end. Under ordinary circumstances his election to the office of United States Senator would not have interfered with this pledge."

But something unexpected happened. A special early session of the U.S. Senate was called, and Booth was expected to attend. Still, the governor remained reluctant, considering the possibility of waiting for the regular session of the Senate to convene before going to Washington D.C.

If Booth did not heed the early call, the Chronicle speculated, he faced a possible constitutional legality in qualifying as a U.S. Senator.

"This question is now being considered by Governor Booth and certain legal friends whom he has called into consultation," the newspaper reported. The Chronicle was convinced that Booth was making much ado about nothing by trying to hang on to the governor's chair until the last possible moment.

"The political and personal friendship existing between the Governor and the Lieutenant Governor, and their accord upon all questions of public trust, makes the matter of resignation but one of secondary importance," said the Chronicle. The news story also included something that must have gladdened Pacheco's heart: "Our own opinion has been expressed..that Governor Booth should not hesitate to present himself to Washington.." (66)

*****

Romualdo Pacheco Becomes Governor

Then, at long last, on February 28, 1875, the newspaper carried a short story on an inside page reporting, "Governor Booth has resigned his position as chief magistrate of California, and he will fill his position in the Senate of the United States upon its opening on the 5th of the next month.

"Romualdo Pacheco has been sworn in as acting governor..The lieutenant governor will bring to the position a large experience gained by a long and intimate knowledge of our state affairs. His high personal

ROMUALDO PACHECO'S CALIFORNIA

character is a guarantee of the faithful and intelligent performance of the duties of his office. Mr. Irwin of Siskiyou, as president of the senate, becomes lieutenant governor and exofficio warden of the state prison." (67)

The transition was quiet. The legislature was not in session, so no new bills could be passed during the next ten months while Pacheco, the twelfth governor in the American period, served. But he surely knew even then that the real significance of what had happened lay in his extraordinary historical achievement. At this writing, he is the only hispanic who ever served as governor of the state of California during the American period.

****

Epilogue

When the state political parties gathered at the end of the year to nominate officials for elective office, Pacheco's hometown newspaper, the Tribune, supported him for governor, but he received very little positive help from the large city newspapers. At the convention, the Republicans ignored him. (68)

The Independent Party did not consider him for governor, but again nominated him for lieutenant governor. However, the whole Independent movement was swamped in that election. Democrat William Irwin, presiding officer of the Senate and lieutenant governor under Pacheco was elected governor.

That might have been the end of Pacheco's political career, but the Republicans soon called him back to duty. On August 10, 1876, the fourth congressional district Republican convention meeting in San Francisco nominated him as their candidate for the United States House of Representatives. "In a rather unique election, he defeated

RECALLING GOVERNOR ROMUALDO Pacheco's beginnings as a half-orphan in the Santa Barbara pueblo. (Jo Mora for Dawn of the Dons by Tirey Ford, 1926.)

THE MEXICAN-AMERICAN WHO WON

the Democratic incumbent, Peter D. Wigginton by..one vote," Melendy said. "It was so close that the Secretary of State refused to grant a certificate of election." However, the State Supreme Court intervened and required that it be done.

Congressman Romualdo Pacheco officially took office at the first session of the 45th Congress, appointed to the committee on public lands. For him, this was a time of learning, but in the second session, he introduced four bills. Only one became law. Throughout the term, he faced the cruel fact that his days might be numbered. Wigginton continued to contest the election. In a vote of the House that reflected party lines, Pacheco was finally unseated February 7, 1878. Whether purposely dealt with in this way or not, his fellow congressmen had divided the term almost equally between Pacheco and Wigginton.

Now that Congressman Pacheco had tasted national politics, he did not give up. He ran for election to Congress again, and on September 7, 1879, he enjoyed a clear victory over Wallace Leach and James J. Ayers, candidates of the Democratic and Workingmen's parties respectively. In that session he again served on the committee for private land claims.

In the third session, he delivered an address seeking funds for the breakwater at Wilmington. Since the Southern Pacific Railroad coastal line had not yet been built, this part of California needed adequate ports for shipping and receiving goods and transporting passengers. In spite of his best efforts, the measure failed.

He again ran for and was elected Congressman in 1881, this time defeating Wallace Leach, his former Democratic opponent, by a

RECALLING GOVERNOR ROMUALDO Pacheco's days of working with the vaqueros on the Canada de Los Osos Rancho in San Luis Obispo County. (Jo Mora for Dawn of the Dons by Tirey Ford, 1926.)

ROMUALDO PACHECO'S CALIFORNIA

small margin.

In the first session of the 47th Congress, he addressed the House, this time urging their favorable vote for a Chinese exclusion bill. His constituents and the California legislature feared the continued influx of Chinese immigrants.

Years before, Governor Booth had summed up prevailing opinion on the west coast: "Because Chinese immigration does not assimilate with our own to form one body of people, it does not meet the conditions which have led the country to invite immigration from Europe. We cannot be blind to the fact that continued immigration of Chinese labor will modify the character of the country..change the relationship between labor and capital. Chinese immigration makes labor merely a cost..down grades the value of manhood..destroys individualism."

Even the most racially tolerant legislators of the time viewed Chinese immigration and cheap labor as destructive. Both legislative branches passed the exclusion bill, but like other chief executives before and after him, President Chester Arthur saw China as a great potential market for American manufactured goods. He did not want to close this door. He vetoed the bill.

Pacheco devoted most of his time as a legislator to supporting legislative needs of Californians, but out of fifty bills he introduced, only two passed. (69)

After his term ended in 1883, he did not run for public office again. However, on December 11, 1890, President Benjamin Harrison appointed him Envoy Extraordinary and Minister Plenipotentiary to Central America. It was a fitting recognition for a lifetime of service to his country. During 1891, he presented his credentials in the capitals of Guatemala, El Salvador, Honduras, Costa Rica and Nicaragua.

After a brief return to California in 1892, he again sailed to Guatemala and Honduras on diplomatic missions. However, on this occasion, members of Alcatraz Parlor 145 of the Native Sons of the Golden West saw him off at the Pacific Mail dock in San Francisco. This acclamation marks a small irony in the Americanization of the Hon. Romualdo Pacheco. He had been governor of California at the

Recalling the days of Mexican California when a wooden-wheeled carreta pulled by horned steers was the principal mode for hauling. (Jo Mora for Dawn of the Dons by Tirey Ford, 1926.)

THE MEXICAN-AMERICAN WHO WON

time the Native Sons was formed, but was not considered eligible because he was a California-born citizen of the Mexican period. Sometime later, the organization changed the rule. (70)

Library of Congress files provide a variety of telegraphed instructions from the state department as well as reports from Envoy Romualdo Pacheco while he served in Central America. (71)

He continued his service as envoy until President Harrison's term of office ended.

Back in private life, Pacheco tried a variety of occupations, including working for an investment firm and raising cattle in Mexico. His family's lands in San Luis Obispo County had long since passed into other hands.

Pacheco died at the home of his brother-in-law, Henry R. Miller, in Oakland January 23, 1899.

Throughout his life, Romualdo Pacheco possessed the same courage and strong will of many of his Californio forebears who enjoyed success. Along the way, he also received support from many Americans. In his wisdom, he drew upon the best qualities of all who influenced him.

"The body (of Romualdo Pacheco) was escorted to St. Pauls Episcopal Church then located at 14th and Harrison Streets, by members of the Masonic Order," Peter Thomas Comny of the Natives Sons recorded. "There were ten honorary pallbearers, including two from the Native Sons and two from the California Society of Pioneers."

Among the honorary pallbearers was San Francisco capitalist Lloyd Tevis, father-in-law of Pacheco's daughter, Maybella. Others serving included General Shafter, Mark Sheldon, Judge McSweeney, Gordon Blakely and N. W. Spaulding. (72)

Henry Gage, the Governor of California, sent a military escort to the funeral. Following the Episcopal services, Pacheco's body was interred in Oakland's Mountain View Cemetery.

****

Recalling the traditional rodeos of Mexican California. (Jo Mora for Dawn of the Dons by Tirey Ford, 1926)

SAN JOSE FIRST SITE OF STATE CAPITOL-1849-51

CHOOSING CALIFORNIA'S CAPITOL SITE

San Jose was the first settlement founded and established by the Spanish government as a city quite independent of any mission or presidio.

In November, 1777, California Governor Felipe de Neve brought 14 soldiers and their families from the presidios of Monterey and San Francisco, founding and settling a new pueblo they named San Jose de Guadalupe. San Jose became an agricultural town, a characteristic that later appealed to the members of California's Constitutional Convention in Monterey during the Fall of 1849. At this meeting, San Jose offered 31 acres of land and a meeting place for the new legislature. The delegates quickly accepted this offer.

Unfortunately, it was very rainy in San Jose when the legislators gathered December 15, 1849. They found themselves "wallowing in mud" and fighting a flea infestation. The adobe building where they met was unfinished and the retail stores, hotels, restaurants and bars charged outrageous prices. Lawmakers were scarcely in the mood for conducting

THE MEXICAN-AMERICAN WHO WON

VALLEJO SECOND SITE OF CAPITOL-1852-53

the state's business. They became known that year as "the legislature of a thousand drinks."

A marker designates the location of this building in the 100 block of South Market street.

Because the legislature was not comfortable about making San Jose the permanent capital, General Vallejo, now a state senator, seized the opportunity to present a deal. He offered 156 acres and $370,000 for construction of state buildings on his land along San Pablo Bay. The legislators were overwhelmed and gratefully accepted his generous offer.

So, on January 5, 1852, the next legislative body arrived in the new town of Vallejo and looked around. What they saw must have left them feeling very dismal. There was a small unfinished meeting hall, and the streets of the town were mere paths. Cattle roamed at will, using the whole settlement for pasture.

The legislators tried to conduct business in Vallejo for about one week. Then, lobbyists from Sacramento came to their rescue, inviting them to continue the 1952 session in their new county courthouse at Sacramento.

In January, 1853, the legislators again returned to Vallejo. But things had not changed much. A state historical marker designates the original

ROMUALDO PACHECO'S CALIFORNIA

BENICIA-THIRD SITE OF CAPITOL, 1853-54

location of the building at 219 York Street.

When the Vallejo settlement did not meet expectations, the community of Benicia, named for Francisca Benicia, Vallejo's wife, offered "the gratuitous use of its city hall as a statehouse." Hastily, the little town suitably furnished the building. It also built a boardwalk along the muddy street between the hall and the business section of town. In 1853, legislators conducted the state's business in what was now the third city to serve as a meeting place.

The Benicia hall was a small handsome two-story brick building with white Doric columns dignifying the entrance. It provided four comfortable committee rooms and a newly carpeted Senate chamber on the first floor. Almost the entire second floor served as the Assembly Room.

The people of Benicia arranged an elegant welcoming ball in the Assembly Room and brought in about 30 unmarried women as dance partners. Absolutely nothing went wrong that year.

So, the legislature returned to Benicia again in January, 1854. But everyone knew that a movement was underway by Sacramento to return the legislators to their city. The capitol structure now stands at the corner of First and G streets.

THE MEXICAN-AMERICAN WHO WON

SACRAMENTO CHOSEN PERMANENT SITE FOR CAPITOL IN 1854

Sacramento lobbyists enjoyed a great deal of power in 1854. Governor John Bigler was himself a resident of Sacramento. He not only offered free rent at the new county courthouse, but a city square for construction of a state capitol. Before the session ended, the governor signed a bill making Sacramento the permanent site of state government.

REFERENCES

1. Bancroft, Hubert- CALIFORNIA PIONEER INDEX, 1542-1848. Regional Publishing Co., Baltimore, 1964. Pages 128, 272, 370.

2. Bancroft, Hubert- HISTORY OF CALIFORNIA, Vol. II, page 788; Vol. III, pages 204-206; 650. Also see Angel, Myron- HISTORY OF SAN LUIS OBISPO COUNTY, Page 290.

3. Melendy, H. Brett and Gilbert, Benjamin F.- THE GOVERNORS OF CALIFORNIA, The Talisman Press, Georgetown, 1965. Page 167.

4. Bancroft, Pioneer Index.

5. Bancroft, Pioneer Index.

6. Bancroft, Pioneer Index.

7. Bancroft, Pioneer Index.

8. Dana, R. H. Jr.-TWO YEARS BEFORE THE MAST, Fields, Osgood and Company, Boston, 1869. Page 126.

9. Letter from Faxon Dean Atherton, Valparaiso, to Thomas Oliver Larkin, dated August 10, 1843. The Larkin Papers, Vol. II, Page 31. Published by Bancroft Library, University of California Press, Berkeley and Los Angeles, 1952. Original letter at Huntington Library, San Marino, California. Henceforth referred to as the Larkin Papers.

10. Guillerno Carrillo and his family lived in this casa later, and it became known as Casa de Carrillo. In 1930, it was given to the Santa Barbara Foundation. It is now beautifully restored and open to the public at 11 East Carrillo Street, Santa Barbara.

11. Gudde, Erwin Gustav, translator and editor- "Edward Vischer's First Visit to California." California Historical Society Quarterly, Vol. 19, Page 201.

12. Green, Edward Craft- "Journal of Captain John Paty, 1807-1868." California Historical Society Quarterly, Vol. XIX, Number 4, Page 325.

13. Judd, Bernice; Sexton, Audrey B.; Wilcox, Barbara S.; Alexander, Elizabeth G.- MISSION ALBUM, Sesquicentennial Edition, 1820-1970. Page 127.

14. Letter from Thomas Oliver Larkin, Monterey, to Andrew Johnstone, Honolulu dated August 27, 1840. Larkin Papers, Vol 1, Page 50. Original letter in Huntington Library, San Marino.

15. A brief history of the school is available from the Septennial Report, Oahu Charity School, 1841 at the Library of the Mission Houses Museum in Honolulu.

16. "The Sandwich Islands," from Richard B. Hinds JOURNAL OF THE VOYAGE OF THE SULPHUR (1836-1842), Hawaiian Journal of History, Vol. II, 1968. Provides insightful information about social conditions in Honolulu in 1837. On July 10, 1841, a year when Romualdo Pacheco attended, Hinds visited the Oahu Charity School.

17. Comny, Peter Thomas, director of historical research, Grand Parlor of the Native Sons of the Golden West: "Romualdo Pacheco, 1831-1899. Distingushed Californian of the Mexican and American Periods." Henceforth referred to as Comny.

18. Letter from Faxon Dean Atherton, Valparaiso, to Thomas Oliver Larkin, Monterey, dated August 10, 1843. Vol. II, Page 31, Larkin Papers.

19. Letter from John Coffin Jones, Oahu, to Thomas Oliver Larkin, Monterey, dated May 10, 1844, Vol. 2, Page 118, Larkin Papers.

THE MEXICAN-AMERICAN WHO WON

20. United States Land Commission Records, Southern District- Mission San Luis Obispo. Nicholson, Loren- "Captain John Wilson, Trader of the Pacific." See also U.S. Land Commission Case 28 SD- Transcript of Recordings in the Petition for Canada de Los Osos and Pecho y Islay, John Wilson, claimant. Granted September 24, 1845. Other land cases: Canada del Chorro, Case 25 SD, granted October 10, 1845, judicial possession, May 15, 1946; Huerta de Romualdo, Cases 50, 261 SD, patented April 13, 1871; Mission San Luis Obispo, 366 SD, granted December, 6, 1845.

21. Comny, Page 5, 6

22. Original letter from Romualdo Pacheco, San Luis Obispo, to Abel Stearns, San Pedro dated June 18, 1853. Abel Stearns Papers, Huntington Library, San Marino.

23. Bancroft, Pioneer Index, Page 172.

24. Angel, Myron- HISTORY OF SAN LUIS OBISPO, Howell-North Books, Berkeley, 1966. Pages 135-136.

25. Bancroft, Pioneer Index, Pages 365-367.

26. Angel, Page 131.

27. Angel, Page 134.

28. Angel, Page 135.

29. Angel, Page 136

30. THE SAN LUIS OBISPO COUNTY COURT INDEX, 1853-1857, and the Levey vs. Wilson Case recorded November 8, 1854, Judge Romualdo Pacheco presiding.

31. Angel, Page 142.

32. Angel, Page 297.

33. Original letter written by Walter Murray to his sister, Anne, in England, dated May 28, 1858. Walter Murray Papers, Bancroft Library, University of California, Berkeley, California.

34. Angel, Page 298.

35. Angel, Page 299.

36. Dana, 442.

37. Angel, Page 286.

38. John Wilson Probate Papers- In a document dated March 27, 1891, A. M. Graves, now the administrator of the Wilson estate, reviewed the circumstances in the distribution of the Wilson property since the latter's death. Ramona, Romualdo's mother, had died December 16, 1886 in San Francisco. Source: San Luis Obispo County Clerk's Office, San Luis Obispo.

39. Undated letter from Sarah Murray, London, to Alexander Murray, San Luis Obispo. Original letter, Walter Murray Papers, Bancroft Library, University of California, Berkeley. Typewritten copy available in Special Collections, California Polytechnic State University Library, San Luis Obispo.

40. John Wilson Probate Papers- See above reference 39.

41. John Wilson Probate Papers- See above reference 39.

42. Comny, Page 8.

43. Angel, Page 150; Bancroft Pioneer Index, pages 287, 367.

44. Angel, Page 149.

45. Melendy, Page 168; Comny, Pages 11, 12.

46. Comny, Page 13.

47. Melendy, page 168; Comny, Page 8.

48. Bancroft, Pioneer Index, Page 108

49. Angel, Page 152

50. Angel, Pages 32 (a,b,c)

51. San Luis Obispo Tribune, August 7, 1869.

52. Angel, Pages 153, 154.

53. San Francisco Chronicle, September 10, 1871.

54. San Francisco Chronicle, July 2, 1871.

55. San Francisco Chronicle, July 14, 1871.

56. San Francisco Chronicle, July 2, 1871.

57. San Francisco Chronicle, July 2, 1871.

58. Hittell, Theodore H.- HISTORY OF CALIFORNIA, W. J. Stone & Co., 1898. Vol. IV, Chapter 7, Pages 496-523.

59. San Francisco Chronicle, November 30, 1873.

60. San Francisco Chronicle, December 2, 1873.

61. San Francisco Chronicle, December 2, 1873.

62. San Francisco Chronicle, December 12, 1873.

63. San Francisco Chronicle, December 20, 1873.

64. San Francisco Chronicle, December 21, 1873.

65. Comny, Page 164.

66. San Francisco Chronicle, February 27, 1875.

67. San Francisco Chronicle, February 28, 1875.

EPILOGUE

68. San Luis Obispo Tribune, April 20, 1875.

69. Melendy, Page 171.

70. Melendy, Page 172.

71. Benjamin Harrison Papers, Original Telegram Cyphers at Library of Congress, Washington, D.C. Copies available at the California State Library, Sacramento.
- Telegram, August 10, 1891 from "Wharton, Acting", Department of State, Washington, D.C. to Minister Romualdo Pacheco. Instructions re: City of Panama and San Salvadoran Minister of Foreign Affairs complaint.
- Telegram, August 12, 1891 from Romualdo Pacheco, Guatemala, to "Secretary Blaine", Washington D.C. re: City of Panama detained at La Liberstad.
- Telegram, August 14, 1891 from Minister Romualdo Pacheco, Guatemala, to "Secretary Blaine", Washington D.C.. City of Panama arrives Guatemala. Passengers landed. Cargo discharged at San Jose. Protest to San Salvador telegraphed.
-There were other intermediary telegraphs dispatched in relationship to the City of Panama affair.

72. Comny, page 14.